POTATOES

POTATOES

the definitive cook's guide to the world's best varieties
and how to cook with them

Alex Barker with recipes by Sally Mansfield

LORENZ BOOKS

This edition is published by Lorenz Books

Lorenz Books is an imprint of Anness Publishing Ltd
Hermes House, 88–89 Blackfriars Road, London SE1 8HA
tel. 020 7401 2077; fax 020 7633 9499
www.lorenzbooks.com; info@anness.com

© Anness Publishing Ltd 2000, 2002

Published in the USA by Lorenz Books, Anness Publishing Inc.
27 West 20th Street, New York, NY 10011; fax 212 807 6813

Published in Australia by Lorenz Books, Anness Publishing Pty Ltd
Level 1, Rugby House, 12 Mount Street, North Sydney, NSW 2060
tel. (02) 8920 8622; fax (02) 8920 8633

This edition distributed in the UK by Aurum Press Ltd
25 Bedford Avenue, London WC1B 3AT
tel. 020 7637 3225; fax 020 7580 2469

This edition distributed in the USA by National Book Network
4720 Boston Way, Lanham, MD 20706
tel. 301 459 3366; fax 301 459 1705; www.nbnbooks.com

This edition distributed in Canada by General Publishing
895 Don Mills Road, 400–402 Park Centre, Toronto, Ontario M3C 1W3
tel. 416 445 3333; fax 416 445 5991; www.genpub.com

This edition distributed in New Zealand by David Bateman Ltd
30 Tarndale Grove, Off Bush Road, Albany, Auckland
tel. (09) 415 7664; fax (09) 415 8892

Publisher: Joanna Lorenz
Executive Editor: Linda Fraser
Editor: Rebecca Clunes
Indexer: Hilary Bird
Editorial Reader: Diane Ashmore
Production Controller: Don Campaniello
Designer: Margaret Sadler
Photography: Steve Moss (potatoes) and Sam Stowell (recipes)
Food for Photography: Alex Barker (techniques), Eliza Baird (recipes)
Additional Recipes: Roz Denny, Jacks Clarke, Joanna Farrow, Shirley Gill, Sarah Gates, Steven Wheeler, Hilaire Walden, Christine France, Rosamund Grant, Sheila Kimberley, Liz Trigg, Carla Capalbo, Carole Clements, Judy Jackson, Ruby Le Bois, Chris Ingram, Matthew Drennan, Elizabeth Wolfe-Cohen, Shehzad Hussain, Rafi Fernandez, Manisha Kanini, Laura Washburn, Andi Clevely, Katherine Richmond, Jennie Shapter

Previously published as *Discovering Potatoes*

1 3 5 7 9 10 8 6 4 2

NOTES

For all recipes, quantities are given in both metric and imperial measures and, where appropriate, measures are also given in standard cups and spoons. Follow one set, but not a mixture, because they are not interchangeable.

Standard spoon and cup measures are level. 1 tsp = 5ml, 1 tbsp = 15ml, 1 cup = 250ml/8fl oz

Australian standard tablespoons are 20ml. Australian readers should use 3 tsp in place of 1 tbsp for measuring small quantities of gelatine, cornflour, salt, etc.

Medium eggs are used unless otherwise stated.

CONTENTS

THE POTATO – ITS HISTORY

THERE ARE FEW more important foods in the world than the potato. Its history goes back to the early days of man – a past spanning feast and famine. It has long played a vital role as the best all-round source of nutrition for mankind, and will continue to do so in the future.

The potato was discovered by pre-Inca Indians in the foothills of the Andes Mountains in South America. Archaeological remains have been found dating from 400 BC on the shores of Lake Titicaca, in ruins near Bolivia, and on the coast of Peru. Cultivated by the Incas, it influenced their whole lives. The Peruvian potato goddess was depicted holding a potato plant in each hand. The South American Indians measured time by the length of time it took to cook potatoes to various consistencies. Potato designs were found in Nazca and Chimu pottery. Raw slices of potato placed on broken bones were thought to prevent rheumatism.

The original potatoes, ranging from the size of a nut to a small apple, and ranging in colour from red and gold to blue and black, flourished in these temperate mountain plateaux. The first recorded information about the potato

was written in 1553 by the Spanish conquistador Pedro Cieza de Leon and soon potatoes joined the treasures carried away by these Spanish invaders. They became standard food on Spanish ships, and people began to notice that the sailors who ate them did not suffer from scurvy.

The first known purchase of the potato was by a hospital in Seville in 1573. Its cultivation spread quickly throughout Europe via explorers such as

Above: A ceramic plate made by the Incas, which typically would have been used for serving potatoes

Sir Francis Drake, who is reputed to have brought potatoes back to Britain. These are thought to have been cultivated on Sir Walter Raleigh's estate in Ireland, 40,000 acres of land given to him by Queen Elizabeth I expressly to grow potatoes and tobacco. Botanists and scientists were fascinated by this novel plant – it was mentioned in John Gerard's herbal list in 1597 – and potatoes may first have been grown mainly for botanical research. During Charles II's reign, the Royal Society recognized the potato as being nutritional and inexpensive and, with the ever-present fear of famine and war, governments in Europe tried to persuade their farmers to start growing this valuable crop in quantity.

However the potato also carried with it a reputation. As part of the nightshade family, it was thought to be poisonous or to cause leprosy and syphilis and to be a dangerous aphrodisiac. In France, a young chemist, Antoine Augustin Parmentier, set about converting the French and their King Louis XVI with his potato delicacies (hence his name is now used often in connection with potato dishes), and Marie Antoinette was persuaded to wear potato blossoms in her hair. But in some cases it took more than just

Above: The Golden Hind *in which Sir Francis Drake brought potatoes back to Britain*

Above: The potato flower

in the 1840s. Over a million people died and it is hardly surprising that the potato became known as the white or Irish potato, to distinguish it from the sweet potato.

The Irish took their love of the potato with them when they moved in large numbers to the north of England, as well as to Europe and America to escape the famine. The British government had by now accepted the potato as a nutritious, cheap and easily grown food and were encouraging the use of allotments for potato growing; "potato patches" as they became known in the Victorian era. The fear of another potato crop disaster through disease, along with the new-found appreciation of its table value caused intense interest in improving potato varieties throughout Europe. At the International Potato Show at London's Alexandra Palace in 1879 there were reputed to have been several hundred varieties on show. By the turn of the century the potato was the accepted main vegetable crop and was exported throughout Europe.

POTATOES IN THE WORLD TODAY

Now the potato is the staple food for two-thirds of the world's population and our third most important food crop. It is the best all-round source of nutrition known to man, second only to eggs for protein and better even than soya beans, the protein food of the second half of the 20th century. Growing potatoes is also the world's most efficient means of converting land, water and labour into an edible product – a field of potatoes produces more energy per acre per day than a field of any other crop.

persuasion. King Frederick of Prussia ordered his people to plant potatoes to prevent famine but had to enforce these orders by threatening to cut off the noses and ears of those who refused. European immigrants introduced potatoes to North America but it was not until Irish immigrants took the potato to Londonderry, New Hampshire in 1719, that it began to be grown in any quantity. Early in the 19th century, Lord Selkirk also emigrated with a group from the Isle of Skye in Scotland to settle in an area known as Orwell Point on Prince Edward Island, Canada. With him he took potatoes and the community survived on potatoes and cod for many years.

By the end of the 18th century, the potato was becoming a major crop, particularly in Germany and Britain. The Irish peasants were eating a daily average of ten potatoes per person, 80 per cent of their diet. In addition, potatoes were fodder for their animals who provided their milk, meat and eggs. This total dependence proved to be disastrous for the Irish when the blight of *Phytophthora infestans* struck the potato harvest in three successive years

Above: The great exhibition hall at London's Alexandra Palace

*Above: The sweet potato or yam flower (*Ipomoea batatas*)*

surrato, pompiterre, bombiderre, castanhola (chestnut from Spain) are some of the European ones. Chinese names include *shanyao* (mountain medicine), *didan* (ground egg), *fanzaishu* (potato with many children) and *aierlanshu* (Irish potato), to mention but a few.

THE POTATO PLANT CYCLE

The potato is related to both the tomato and the tobacco plant. Its botanical name is *Solanum tuberosum*, from the *Solanaceae* family, and the only edible part is the tuber. The plant is bushy and sprawling with clusters of dark green leaves. It produces flowers which range in colour from white to purple or striped and occasionally grows yellow-green fruits which contain anything from 100 to 300 kidney-shaped seeds. When grown from seed (or seed potato) it sprouts upwards producing a shoot, and downwards producing a root. The shoot first forms leaves, then flowers and as they die back the excess energy is stored as starch below ground in tubers at the ends of the roots. These tubers, the potatoes, grow larger as more and more starch is produced.

Potato tubers have several small indentations or external buds (as consumers we call them eyes and cut them out before eating them) which, when allowed to grow, form new stems or sprouts. Some of these will successfully grow into new plants using the stored food in the tuber. This original tuber is known as a seed potato which home growers and most commercial growers buy every year. In fact, you only need a piece of potato with one bud in, not even the whole potato, to produce one potato plant.

Producing the plant from seed is a much more complex process. The flower grown from this seed needs pollinating and it is only when this occurs in a controlled environment that you can be sure what the resultant plant will be like. In all the major potato growing countries there are seed potato producers and breeding centres where researchers are constantly developing

Statistics for potato production around the world show up many interesting factors. Russia is still the world's largest potato producer with Poland, China and the USA not far behind them.

Consumption trends, however, are now changing the demands which are put upon potato growers. This is due mainly to the trend towards Mediterranean eating which is heavily based on alternative starch foods, such as pasta and rice. Although potatoes are still a major seller the bulk of those sold

are pre-packed, many in the form of chips. Part of this consumption of chips is in a frozen form, and is worldwide, with America and the Far East setting the trend. Freezing potatoes is certainly not new, however. The early Incas, 2,000 years ago, turned potatoes into a form of convenience food called chuno, by a process of natural freezing and drying which meant they could be kept for much longer.

Throughout the world the potato goes under many other names: *pomme de terre, kartoffel, patata, batateirs, batala*

Above: A selection of rare potatoes, clockwise from top, Mr Bressee, International Kidney, Blue Catriona, Champion, Edgecote Purple, Arran Victory

new breeds. The Netherlands, the USA, Peru and the UK are key centres and, as with rare breeds of animals, the researchers log those that go out of favour or fashion, endeavouring to keep these breeds going for future reference and genetic research. Their main aim, however, is to develop new breeds which will enable more efficient potato production for the various climates throughout the world. These include breeds that can resist viruses and diseases or ones that will store better for longer, and breeds which provide the culinary qualities that certain markets demand, such as being good for chipping and processing. It is rare, of course, that all the desired qualities are found in one plant – in fact on average only one in 100,000 seedlings ever becomes registered as a cultivar (a possible new breed).

Only then does a seed go into field trials and it could be at least another 3–4 years before it is seen on the commercial market. There are several thousand varieties in existence throughout the world therefore, although only a fraction of those are in regular production. Countries with seed potato research centres provide key information annually for their seed producers. In Britain there are about 700 varieties held at the Department of Agriculture and Fisheries for Scotland listed in the Douglas M MacDonald collection. The Potato Association of America classifies up to 4,000 varieties but the International Potato Centre in Peru (CIP) has the largest gene bank, holding 3,694 cultivars.

Although varieties such as Blue Don, Elephant, King Kidney, Perthshire Red, The Howard and Victoria – some dating as far back as the 16th century – have become extinct, other more famous names are in various collections for posterity. These include Congo, a bright blue potato from pre-1900, Edgecote Purple and Champion. Other aged varieties are being revived, through the success of research and supermarket innovation. Names such as Mr Bressee, Blue Catriona and Arran Victory are returning to our shops. Home growers, buying from seed catalogues, now have an even more exciting wealth of new varieties to experiment with.

FROM FIELD TO TABLE

The potato grows in over 180 countries, from an altitude of sea level to 14,000 feet, under a wider range of climatic conditions than any other staple food. It matures faster too, taking from 90 to 140 days. Yet much still depends on the grower knowing his or her potato, finding the right potato for the market and then making the most of the environment – a technology on its own.

Large scale potato production is highly mechanized, from planting to harvesting. Rows of furrows are made in the field by machines, ready for mechanical planters to drop in the seed potatoes. Machines aided by computer determine the depth of the troughs, the spacing of seed potatoes and soil fertilization, monitoring for pests and diseases and crop spraying as well. In good time for harvesting, the plant is left to finally mature and be ready for picking, which is done by machine, several rows at a time. The potatoes, separated from soil and stones by machines and briefly air dried, are stored in insulated boxes in controlled ventilation warehouses. Those going to local market are graded by size or riddled before being bagged or put into sacks.

Above: Grading potatoes by size using a riddling machine

After harvesting, potatoes are stored or cured at a temperature of 15–18°C/59–65°F before being put into long-term storage at a temperature just above freezing. This helps to prevent sprouting but potatoes going into storage for up to ten months may also be sprayed. At these temperatures the potato starch can be affected and turn to sugar, so before processing the potatoes go back into short-term storage at the curing temperature to convert the sugars back to starch. On smaller farms and in areas where farm workers are readily available, many of these jobs are still done partially by hand. In more rural regions potatoes can still sometimes be found stored in clamps where the potatoes are stacked up under piles of soil and straw to keep them dry and frost-free.

Above: The Yanaimilla and the Compis (see below) are descendants of the original South American potatoes

Potatoes are classified by the length of time they take to mature although this can be affected by the weather and the climate. First earlies, also called new potatoes, are planted in early spring for harvesting, after some 100–110 days, in early summer. Second earlies, as the name implies, are planted in late spring and harvested, after 110–120 days, from mid to late summer as late new potatoes. Maincrop potatoes are planted in the spring but not harvested for at least 125–140 days in late summer. These are the potatoes which go into long-term storage for sale in the next season, whilst earlies go straight into the shops.

When a young potato is dug up it has fragile, flaky skin. As it matures the skin sets and after a certain length of time will no longer flake and the flesh becomes much more starchy. Maincrop potatoes have to be kept in the ground maturing as long as possible to produce skins which are thick enough to survive in long-term storage. You will now find that you can buy a young, new Maris Piper for instance, which is small and flaky, at the same time as you can buy the large, firm maincrop Maris Piper, since each may be grown in different areas by different producers.

NUTRITION

The potato is the single most important source of vitamin C for much of the world, in particular the poorer countries where there is little fruit and certainly no other dietary supplements. We all need vitamin C to help fight off infections and to keep muscle, skin and bones healthy. Unlike many vegetables, the entire potato is edible and nutritious, providing important amounts of protein, vitamins and minerals, and it can be cooked in ways to suit most climates, ethnic traditions and cooking abilities. More than that, for the Western societies which are suffering from the excesses of good food, potatoes can provide a useful amount of one of the key elements needed in our modern healthy diet – fibre.

Above: The Compis, like the Yanaimilla, are only grown by local Andean Farmers

The bulk of the potato, about 75 per cent or more according to how you cook it, is made up of water. The largest

Above: Baked potatoes are a valuable source of protein, fibre and vitamin C

amount of the rest – 17 per cent – is starch, known also as complex carbohydrate. Current recommendations for the Western diet suggest that we should get at least 40 per cent of our food energy – our total calorie consumption per day – from starchy foods such as potatoes. One large baked potato, approximately 300g/11oz, will provide about 250 calories. Potatoes also contain 2.1 per cent protein, 1.3 per cent fibre, good quantities of vitamin C, almost no fat and other important trace elements such as foliate (for red blood cells), potassium (which helps calm the nerves) and iron (which helps oxygen travel easily around the body). New potatoes have a particularly high vitamin C content and a 100g/3¾oz serving can provide 23 per cent of our daily requirement.

The way potatoes are stored and cooked also affects their nutritional content. Vitamin C can be lost during long storage in too much light and it can also be lost whilst they are soaking in water before and during the cooking process. Chips, surprisingly, are not such a bad way of cooking potatoes as they are often portrayed. They manage to retain more of the vitamin C because the method of cooking involves less soaking in water and, if oven-baked, 100g/3¾oz chips will actually have fewer calories than 100g/3¾oz of fruit and nut mix.

GROWING YOUR OWN POTATOES

Potatoes usually grow well in most soils, and whether you have a small corner or a large plot, whether you have years of experience or are a novice gardener, they will produce a worthwhile result for relatively little effort. Just 900g/2lb of seed potatoes can give around 23kg/50lb potatoes, so unless you have plenty of storage space or have a large family you may only need to plant a small amount or stagger the harvesting. Early potatoes produce a smaller crop than maincrop potatoes so they also require less space.

PREPARATION

Prepare the ground in the autumn before it gets too hard, clearing the weeds and digging in a good compost or manure, about one bucketful to 1sq m/1.2sq yds. A couple of weeks before planting, dig over the ground adding fertilizers as recommended. Potatoes need a lot of space; a 900g/2lb seed bag will require 0.9–1.2sq m/3–4sq ft of soil for instance. Seed potatoes can be put in trays at the end of January in a cool room or warmed greenhouse, to encourage the sprouts to grow earlier and give a better crop.

PLANTING

In most climates first earlies can be planted from mid-spring; in colder regions wait until late spring.

1 Make drills or shallow trenches about 10cm/4in deep and 45cm/18in apart with a hoe, or up to 60cm/2ft apart for maincrop potatoes, Place the seed potatoes, sprouts uppermost, into them.

2 Fill in the drills with soil, increasing the height of soil over the potato seed for protection.

3 For easier, weed-free growth and frost protection, plant the seeds under black plastic. Secure the edges of the plastic under soil.

4 Make several cross-shaped slits where the potatoes will be planted, making sure they are covered with at least 5cm/2in of soil.

PROTECTING

As the shoots start to appear, draw up more soil over the seed potato into a ridge, giving protection against frost, and continue this earthing-up process every two weeks until the foliage meets between the rows or you have soil mounds about 15cm/6in high. Water occasionally in a very dry spring or more frequently for earlies.

HARVESTING

Early potatoes should be ready for harvesting from early summer in milder climates – as a rough guide after about 12–14 weeks. You could start by carefully pushing away earth from the higher part of the ridges to remove any that are ready. Replace the soil if they are still too small.

Maincrop potatoes, on the other hand, have to be held in the ground until the foliage dies down, so the tubers can keep growing and the skin sets firmly for longer storage. To be sure, lift one or two potatoes, as above, and try rubbing the skin. If it rubs off easily the potatoes are not ready.

1 Dig up the potatoes with a large fork and sort them into groups by size. Leave them on the ground for an hour or two to dry off.

2 Store them in large sacks made of hessian if you can find them, or in string bags. Slatted boxes are suitable too, but use straw to both protect the potatoes from bruising and keep them frost-free and dry. Keep in a dark, cool but not damp place such as a garage, as long as it does not get too cold.

PREPARATION TECHNIQUES

The method you use to prepare your potatoes affects the mineral and vitamin content, and the cooking technique.

CLEANING POTATOES

Most potatoes you buy today are very clean, especially those from supermarkets and pre-packed potatoes, so giving them a light wash will probably be sufficient before boiling them. Locally grown potatoes, farm shop or home-grown potatoes may still have some earth attached to them, so give them a light scrub before cooking. If you are not going to cook them immediately avoid scrubbing the potatoes with water as they can start to go mouldy in warm or damp weather.

1 If the potatoes are very dirty, use a small scrubbing brush or a gentle scourer to clean and remove the peel of the new potatoes.

2 Remove any green or discoloured patches or black eyes carefully, using a pointed knife or potato peeler, unless you are going to peel them after cooking, at which stage they will come out of their skins easily.

PEELING POTATOES

It is well known that much of the goodness and flavour of a potato is in the skin and just below it. You can boil the potatoes and then peel them afterwards when they are cool enough to handle. The taste is much fresher and earthier if they are prepared this way and perfect for eating plain or simply garnished. Leave the skins on occasionally, which gives more taste and added texture, plus a vital source of roughage and fibre to the diet. Save any peelings you have left over for a very healthy version of crisps.

To peel potatoes use a very sharp potato peeler (there are many different varieties to choose from) to remove the thinnest layer possible in long even strips. Place the potatoes in a saucepan of water so they are just covered until ready to cook, but preferably cook them immediately to avoid any loss of vitamin C.

If you cook potatoes in their skins and want to peel them whilst hot ready for eating immediately, hold the hot potato with a fork and then gently peel off the skin – the skin tends to peel more easily while the potatoes are still hot.

SCRAPING POTATOES

Really new potatoes peel very easily, often just by rubbing them in your hands. You can tell a good new potato, when buying them, by how easily the skin rubs or flakes off.

With a small sharp knife scrape away the flaky skin and place in just enough water to cover.

RUMBLING

This wonderfully old-fashioned word refers to a catering machine with a large revolving bowl and rough, grater-like sides. The potatoes rumble around until the skins are eventually scratched or scraped off. There is one product available for the domestic market which peels the potatoes in the same way.

Wash the potatoes, place in the peeler drum with water as directed, then turn on to speed 2–3 and leave for several minutes. Remove any that are peeled and then continue until the rest are ready. Transfer to a pan of cold water ready for cooking. Don't put in more potatoes than recommended or they may come out misshapen.

GRATING BY HAND

Potatoes can be grated before or after cooking, depending on how you will be using them. They are easier to grate after cooking, when they have had time to cool, and can be grated on a large blade straight into the cooking dish or frying pan. Be sure you don't overcook the potatoes, especially if they are floury, as they will just fall to pieces. Floury potatoes are ideal for mashing, while waxy potatoes are a good choice for making rösti or hash.

Raw potatoes exude a surprising amount of starchy liquid that is vital to helping some dishes stick together. Check before you start whether you need to keep this liquid. The recipe should also tell you whether to rinse off the starchy liquid or just dry the potatoes on kitchen paper. Don't grate the potatoes too soon as the flesh quickly begins to turn brown.

Using a standard grater, grate raw potatoes on a board.

Or if you need the liquid, grate into a medium bowl using either the medium or large blade. Squeeze the liquid from the potatoes by hand.

CHOPPING

Potatoes are often required to be chopped for recipes such as salads and dishes using leftovers. If you are cooking them first the best potatoes to choose are the waxy ones which stay nice and firm. They chop most easily when they are cold and peeled.

To chop, cut the potato in half, then half again and again until it is cut up evenly, as small as is required.

DICING

If the recipe calls for dice this means you have to be much more precise and cut the potato into even shaped cubes. This is usually so that all the sides brown neatly or the pieces cook through evenly.

1 To dice, trim the potato into a neat rectangle first (keep the outside pieces for mash, or to add to a soup), then cut the rectangles into thick, even slices.

2 Turn the stack of slices over and cut into thick batons and finally into even cubes of the size needed for the recipe you are using.

SLICING BY HAND

It may not always matter how neatly and evenly you slice your potatoes, but for some dishes it will affect both the appearance of the finished dish and the cooking time. Try to cut all slices the same thickness so that they cook evenly. Use a large knife for the best results, and make sure that it is sharp otherwise it may slip and cause a nasty cut. To make rounder slices cut across the width of the potato, for longer slices cut along the length of the potato. If you need to slice cooked potatoes for a recipe, be sure to slightly undercook them so they don't fall to pieces either in the dish or when slicing, and let them get really cold before handling them. For most casseroles and toppings cut them about 3mm/⅛in thick.

Put the tip of the knife on the work surface or board first, then press the heel of the knife down firmly to create nice even slices.

SLICING WITH A MANDOLINE

A relative of the musical instrument of the same name, the mandoline has several different cutting blades which vary both the size and shape of the cut potato. The blades are fitted into a metal, plastic or wooden framework for ease of use. It can produce slices from very thin to very thick, as well as fluted slices for crinkle-cut style crisps. It's quite a dangerous gadget, and needs handling with respect because of its very sharp blades. You can cut different thicknesses as required, such as, medium thick (about 2–3mm/¹⁄₁₆–¹⁄₈in) for sautéed potato slices and very thin for crisps.

Plain Slices

Fix the blade to the required thickness, then holding the potato carefully slide it firmly up and down or across the blade. Use the handle or gadget that is provided with some versions to hold on to whenever possible.

Crinkle-cut

For crinkle-cut slices cut the potato horizontally down the fluted blade. Take particular care when the potato gets smaller as it is easy to cut one's fingers on the blade.

Waffled Crisps

For the fancy waffled crisps (*pomme gaufrettes*), cut horizontally down the blade, rotating each time you slice to get a lattice effect.

MAKING CRISPS BY HAND

Home-made crisps are the best, but they can be very fiddly if you do not have the right tools for making them. For a large batch slice the potatoes in a food processor, but for a small batch the slicing blade on a standard grater should give thin enough potato slices if you use it carefully. You can also use a sharp knife to make crisps, but you need to be very careful.

Grating Crisps

To make thin crisps, hold a standard grater firmly on a chopping board, placing a damp cloth on the board to anchor the grater to it and prevent it from sliding. Slide the potato down over the slicing blade carefully. Be sure the grater or mandoline has a very sharp blade. Adjust it to the right thickness or, if it's not adjustable, you will find that the harder you press, the thicker the crisps will be.

Slicing Crisps

This method is best if you want to make small quantites of thick crisps. Hold one end of the potato firmly in your hand and cut thin slices – 3mm/¹⁄₈in thick – with a sharp knife, on a chopping board. Slicing crisps with a knife means that it is easier to adjust the thickness. Remember that the thicker the slice, the less oil will be absorbed by the potato during cooking.

MAKING RIBBONS BY HAND

Thin ribbons, which also deep fry into delicious crisps, can be simply cut with a potato peeler. (Any leftover odd shapes can go into the stockpot.)

To make ribbons, peel the potato like an apple to give very long strips. Work quickly, or put the ribbons in a bowl of cold water as you go, to prevent them turning brown.

CHIPS

The French give their chips various names, depending on how thin or thick they are cut. The larger you cut them the healthier they will be, since they will absorb less fat during the cooking. You can also make chips with their skins on, giving additional fibre.

Traditional English Chips

Use the largest chipping potatoes and cut the potatoes into 1.5cm/⅝in thick slices, or thicker if you wish.

Turn the slices on their side and cut into 1.5cm/⅝in batons, or slightly thicker or thinner if you prefer.

Chip Wedges

For a healthier alternative cut your chips, extra thick, into wedge shapes. First cut the potatoes in half lengthwise, then into long thin wedges.

Pommes Frites

Cut as for chips but slice again into neat, even batons about 6mm/⅛in thick, either by hand or machine.

Pommes Allumettes

Cut the potato into a neat rectangle by removing the rounded sides, then into thin slices and julienne strips about half the thickness of *pommes frites*.

Pommes Pailles (Straw Chips)

Cut the potatoes as for *pommes allumettes* into even finer julienne strips. They are usually pan fried.

Chip-cutter Chips

Chips can be cut with a special chip cutter (see equipment section) and some mandolines. Cut the potatoes to a suitable size to fit.

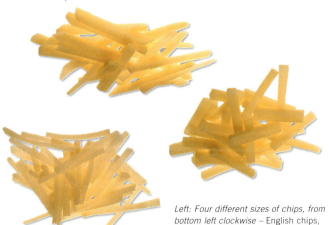

Left: Four different sizes of chips, from bottom left clockwise – English chips, pommes pailles, pommes frites, pommes allumettes

HASSELBACK AND FAN POTATOES

Children often refer to these as hedgehogs as they look quite spiky when roasted to a crispy, golden brown. Peel and dry the potatoes then slice as shown, brush with oil and then put them to roast as soon as possible before they begin to discolour.

To make hasselback potatoes, cut large potatoes in half and place cut side down on a board. With a sharp knife, cut very thin slices across the potato from end to end, slicing deep but not quite through the potato.

To make potato fans, use medium potatoes of long or oval shape and cut them at a slight angle, slicing almost but not quite through the potato, keeping the back section still attached. Press the potato gently on the top until it flattens and fans out at the same time. If you have not cut far enough through it will not fan very much, but if you have cut too far it will split into sections. The best way to cook both these potatoes is to cook them with melted butter and oil and roast them in the oven, preheated to 190°C/375°F/ Gas 5, for 40–50 minutes.

SHAPED POTATOES

Occasionally it is fun to spend the time making potatoes into an artistic creation. You might try these out with children when you are encouraging them to get more involved with preparing and cooking family meals. Use the offcuts for making mash or to thicken soups.

To make potato balls use large firm potatoes for the best results. Peel them and then using a large round or shaped melon baller push it firmly into the potato, twist, and ease out the potato shape. Keep in water until ready to cook, pat dry on kitchen paper and roast or sauté as usual.

To make turned potatoes, first peel small to medium firm potatoes (or quartered large potatoes), trim the ends flat and then cut or trim with a small knife into rugby ball shapes 2.5–5cm/ 1–2in long.

To make potato wedges, cut potatoes in half lengthways, then into quarters and then into eighths. Brush with oil and oven roast or deep fry. The larger the pieces of potato the less fat they will absorb.

PREPARING POTATOES BY MACHINE

Some machines will do many of the jobs already mentioned, such as peeling, grating, slicing, chipping and puréeing, with great speed but not with the precision of your own hands. To get the best results, always cut the potatoes to the same size, use the slowest speed or pulse so you can control the results, and cook the cut potatoes immediately or rinse and dry on kitchen paper to prevent browning.

Home-cooked chips are always the best kind, and cutting them by hand can be time consuming. So use a machine to prepare them for cooking. Fit the correct blade attachment and pack sufficient potatoes in the tube of the food processor so they can be pushed down. Turn on to the slowest speed and press the potato down with the plunger. The harder you press the plunger the thicker the chips will be.

They may turn out slightly bent but that won't affect the taste. For nice evenly sliced potatoes change the attachment on the machine and pack the potatoes so that they will remain facing the same direction and continue as above.

COOKING TECHNIQUES

There are endless different ways of cooking potatoes. However, the best technique depends on both the potato variety and the dish you are cooking.

BLANCHING

Potatoes are blanched (part-cooked) to soften the skin for easy peeling, to remove excess starch for certain recipes and to par-cook before roasting. Use a draining spoon or basket to remove large pieces of potato but when cooking smaller potatoes, place the potatoes in a chip basket for easy removal.

Place the prepared potatoes in a pan of cold water. Bring slowly to the boil and boil gently for 2–5 minutes depending on their size, then drain and use or leave in the cooling water until required.

BOILING

This is the simplest way of cooking potatoes. Place potatoes of a similar size, either whole or cut into chunks, with or without skins (sweet potatoes are best cooked in their skins to retain their bright colour) in a pan with sufficient water just to cover them. Sprinkle on 5–10ml/1–2 tsp salt or to taste, and bring slowly to the boil. Floury potatoes need very gentle boiling or you may find the outside is cooked before the inside is ready and they will become mushy or fall apart in the pan. New potatoes, which have a higher vitamin C content, should be put straight into boiling water and cooked for about 15 minutes and not left soaking. Very firm salad potatoes can be put into boiling water, simmered for

5–10 minutes and then left to stand in the hot water for another 10 minutes until required.

1 Place the potatoes in a large pan and just cover with salted water and a tight-fitting lid. Bring to the boil and leave to gently boil for 15–20 minutes depending on the size and type of potato. Boiling too fast tends to cook the potato on the outside first so it becomes mushy and falls apart before the middle is cooked.

2 When they are finished cooking, drain the potatoes through a colander and then return them to the pan to dry off, as wet or soggy potatoes are not very appetizing.

3 For really dry, peeled potatoes (for mashing for instance), leave them over a very low heat so any moisture can escape. In the north of England they sprinkle the potatoes with salt and shake occasionally until the potatoes stick to the sides of the pan.

4 In Ireland the potatoes are wrapped in a clean tea towel until ready to serve dry and fluffy.

STEAMING

All potatoes steam well but this gentle way of cooking is particularly good for very floury potatoes and those which fall apart easily. Small potatoes, such as new potatoes, steamed in their skins taste really delicious. Make sure potatoes are cut quite small, in even-size chunks or thick slices. Leaving cooked potatoes over a steaming pan of water is also a good way to keep them warm for several minutes.

1 Place prepared potatoes in a sieve, colander or steamer over a deep pan of boiling salted water. Cover as tightly as possible and steam for 5–7 minutes if sliced or cut small, increasing the time to 20 minutes or more if the potatoes are quite large.

2 Towards the end of the cooking time, test a few of the potatoes with a sharp knife, and when cooked, turn off the heat and leave until you are ready to serve them.

3 As an alternative, place a handful of fresh mint leaves in the bottom of the steamer before cooking. The flavour of the mint will penetrate during cooking.

FRYING

The key to successful frying is good fat. A mixture of butter and oil gives good flavour yet allows a higher cooking temperature than just butter.

Shallow Frying

Use a heavy-based large frying pan to allow an even distribution of heat and sufficient room to turn the food.

1 Heat about 25g/1oz/2 tbsp butter and 30ml/2 tbsp oil until bubbling. Put an even layer of cooked or par-cooked potatoes in the hot fat taking care not to splash yourself. Leave for 4–5 minutes until the undersides turn golden.

2 Turn the potatoes over gently with a large fish slice once or twice during cooking until golden brown all over.

Deep Frying

When deep frying, whether you use oil or solid fat, be sure it is fresh and clean. The chips must be well dried as water can cause the fat to bubble up dangerously. Always fry in small batches so the temperature does not drop too much when you add the food and it can cook and brown evenly. Remove any burnt pieces after each batch as this can taint the fat.

To deep fry chips, fill either a chip pan, a deep heavy saucepan with tight-fitting lid, or a deep-fat fryer, about half full with clean fat. Heat to the required temperature by setting the thermostat or test if the oil is hot enough by dropping in a piece of bread; it should turn golden in one minute.

When making chips they are best "blanched" first in hot fat to cook through and seal them without browning. These can then be removed, drained and frozen when cool. Give them a final cooking when you are almost ready to eat, to crisp them up and turn them golden brown.

1 Before frying, dry the chips very thoroughly in a cloth or kitchen paper. Any water or moisture will make the fat splash and spit.

2 Heat the basket in the fat first, then add the chips to the basket (don't overfill or they will not cook evenly), and lower slowly into the pan. If the fat appears to bubble up too much remove the basket and cool the fat slightly.

3 Shake the pan of chips occasionally to allow even cooking, and cook until they are crisp and golden. Remove with a draining spoon or chip basket and drain well against the side of the pan first.

4 Tip the chips on to kitchen paper to get rid of the excess fat before serving, sprinkled with salt.

Deep frying temperatures

- To blanch and seal chips 160°C/325°F
- To quickly fry fine straw chips and crisps and to second cook chips 190°C/375°F

Potato Baskets

1 Cut potatoes into thin, even slices and dry on kitchen paper without rinsing. You will need two wire potato baskets or ladles. Line the larger one evenly with overlapping slices, covering the base well, then clamp the smaller basket inside this one.

2 Slowly immerse in very hot fat for 3–4 minutes until starting to turn golden brown.

3 Remove from the heat, separate the ladles and ease out the basket. Drop back into the fat for another 1–2 minutes until golden.

4 Serve filled with vegetables, stir-fried meat, or sweet and sour prawns.

Safe deep frying

- Never overfill the pan, with either fat or food.
- Always use a tight-fitting lid.
- Have ready a large, very thick cloth to throw over the pan in case of fire.
- NEVER throw water on to a chip pan full of hot or burning fat as it will explode.

BAKING

One of the most comforting and economical meals is a salt-crusted potato baked in its jacket with a fluffy centre that is golden with melted butter and cheese.

Sweet potatoes can be cooked in exactly the same way, sprinkled with a little demerara sugar and topped with soured cream and crispy bacon.

Allow a 275–350g/10–12oz potato for a good size portion and choose the ones recommended for baking, such as Marfona, Maris Piper, Cara or King Edward. Cook in the middle of a hot oven at 220°C/425°F/Gas 7 for 1–1½ hours for very large potatoes or 40–60 minutes for medium potatoes. To test that they are cooked, squeeze the sides gently to make sure that they are sufficiently soft.

1 Wash and dry baking potatoes thoroughly then rub with good oil and add a generous sprinkling of salt. Cook on a baking tray as above.

2 To speed up cooking time and to ensure even cooking throughout, cook the baking potatoes on a skewer, or on special potato baking racks.

3 When really tender cut a cross in the top of each potato and set aside to cool slightly.

4 Hold the hot potato in a clean cloth and squeeze gently from underneath to open up.

5 Place the open potatoes on individual serving plates and pop a lump of butter in each one.

6 For a quick and simple topping, add a little grated tangy Cheddar or similar hard cheese, or a dollop of soured cream and some chopped fresh herbs, such as chives, parsley or coriander. Season with plenty of salt and ground black pepper.

Baked Potato Skins

Bake the potatoes at 220°C/425°F/Gas 7 for 1–1½ hours for large potatoes and 40–60 minutes for medium. Cut in half and scoop out the soft centres. (Mash for a supper or a pie topping.)

Brush the skins with melted butter, margarine or a mixture of butter and oil and return to the top of the oven, at the same temperature, for 20 minutes or until really crisp and golden.

Potato Parcels

Baking a potato in a foil or greaseproof paper parcel, or in a roasting bag, makes for a very tasty potato with no mess and no dirty dishes, if you're careful. If you leave the potatoes in their skins you could prepare them well in advance and put them in to cook in an automatic oven before you get home.

Wash or scrub and dry small potatoes, then wrap them up in a parcel with several knobs of butter, a sprinkle of seasoning and a sprig or two of mint, tarragon or chives. Bake at 190°C/375°F/Gas 5 for about 40–50 minutes for 450g/1lb potatoes.

COOKING IN A CLAY POT

This is most like cooking in a bonfire or under a pile of earth – but here the potatoes take on a deep woody aroma and intense flavour without all the charring and smoke. The terracotta potato pot takes a generous 450g/1lb of potatoes easily. As with all clay pot utensils it should be soaked for 10–20 minutes before using. Use small, even-size potatoes, preferably in their skins. Always place the pot in a cold oven and let the temperature gradually increase to 200°C/400°F/Gas 6. Cook for 40–50 minutes and then test with a pointed knife to see if they are ready.

1 Put the prepared potatoes in the clay pot, toss in 30–45ml/2–3 tbsp of good, preferably extra virgin olive oil or melted butter and sprinkle with roughly ground salt from a mill and pepper. Add your favourite flavourings, such as one large unpeeled clove of garlic, a thick piece of streaky smoked bacon, chopped, or fresh herbs.

2 Put the covered pot in the cold oven and allow to heat to 200°C/400°F/Gas 6. After 40–50 minutes test with a knife. Serve straight from the pot.

MICROWAVED POTATOES

Baking potatoes in the microwave is an enormous time saver, as long as you don't expect the crunchy crust of oven-cooked potatoes. New potatoes and potato pieces can be cooked very quickly and easily. In both cases prick the potato skins first, to prevent bursting. To bake, allow 4–6 minutes per potato, with the setting on a high temperature, increasing by 2–4 minutes for every additional potato. As a guide for smaller boiled potatoes, allow 10–12 minutes per 450g/1lb of cut potatoes on high, or follow the manufacturer's instructions.

Place large potatoes in a circle on kitchen paper on the microwave tray, make cuts around the middle so the skins don't burst and turn once during the cooking process.

Place small potatoes in a microwave bowl with 30–45ml/2–3 tbsp boiling water. Cover tightly with microwave film and pierce two or three times to allow steam to escape during cooking. Leave for 3–5 minutes before draining, adding a knob or two of butter, seasoning and a sprig of mint.

Alternatively, cover the potatoes with a close-fitting microwave lid and cook them using the same method as for the microwave film covered bowl.

Standing time

Allow sufficient standing time afterwards so the potatoes are evenly cooked. Large, baked potatoes should be left to stand for 10 minutes wrapped in serviettes. This will keep them warm before serving and ensure even cooking.

PRESSURE-COOKING

If you want baked potatoes or large potatoes to be cooked in a hurry, or if you want to make a quick and easy mash, this is an ideal cooking method, but it's important to make sure you do not to overcook them, otherwise the potatoes will become dry and floury. Follow the instructions in your manual and allow up to 12 minutes cooking time for large whole potatoes; less for smaller ones. You can cook the potatoes in their skins, which speeds up the process further. Once the potatoes are ready, carefully reduce steam pressure so that they do not overcook.

ROASTING

Melt-in-the-mouth crisp roasties are what Sundays were meant for, so here are some pointers to make sure you get them right every time.

For soft, fluffy-centred roast potatoes, you need to use large baking potatoes – Wilja, Maris Piper, Record, Désirée and Kerr's Pink all give excellent results. Peel (you can roast potatoes in their skins but you won't get the crunchy result most people love), and cut into even-size pieces. Blanch for 5 minutes, then leave in the cooling water for a further 5 minutes to par-cook evenly. Drain well and return to the pan to dry off completely. Well-drained potatoes with roughed up surfaces produce the crispiest results.

A successful roast potato also depends on the fat you cook them in and the temperature. Beef dripping gives the best flavour, although goose fat, if you are lucky enough to find some, is delicious and gives a very light, crisp result. With other roasts you can use lard or, where possible, drain off enough dripping from the joint. A vegetarian alternative is a light olive oil, or olive and sunflower oils mixed.

The fat in the tin must be hot enough to seal the potato surfaces immediately. Use a large enough roasting pan so that you have room to turn the potatoes at least once. Don't leave the almost cooked potatoes in too much fat as they will become soggy. Serve as soon as they are ready for maximum crispness.

1 Blanch the peeled chunks of potato and drain, then shake in the pan or fork over the surfaces to rough them up.

2 Pour a shallow layer of your chosen fat into a good heavy roasting tin and place it in the oven, heating it to a temperature of 220°C/425°F/Gas 7. Add the dry, forked potatoes and toss immediately in the hot oil. Return to the top shelf of the oven and roast for up to one hour.

3 Once or twice during cooking remove the roasting tin from the oven and, using a spatula, turn the potatoes over to evenly coat them in fat. Then drain off any excess fat so they can crisp up and brown more easily.

Flavourings

Flavourings you could try are:
- Curry powder mixes.
- Ground hazelnuts or other nuts.
- Dry seasoning mixes such as Italian Garlic Seasoning or Cajun Seasoning.
- Sesame seeds.
- Garlic and herb breadcrumbs.
- Grated Parmesan cheese.

Healthy Wedges

As a healthier alternative to deep-fried chips and roasties, serve wedges of dry-roasted potatoes sprinkled with various seasonings. Bake at 190°C/375°F/Gas 5, turning often until golden and crisp.

1 Cut large baking potatoes into long thin wedges. Toss in a small amount of very hot sunflower oil in a roasting tin.

2 Sprinkle on seasonings, turn the wedges over several times and bake for 30–40 minutes, turning and testing once or twice.

MASHING AND PURÉEING

The ubiquitous mashed potato has seen a revival in recent years, from a favourite comfort food into a fashion food purely by the addition of olive oil or Parmesan cheese. Every chef and every trendy restaurant today produces their own version. It shows what can be done with a simple ingredient, but you've got to start with good mash. When choosing your potatoes remember that floury potatoes produce a light fluffy mash, while waxy potatoes will result in a dense, rather gluey purée which needs lots of loosening up. Boil even-size potatoes until very well cooked but not falling apart and dry them well, as watery potatoes will give a soggy, heavy mixture. Cold potatoes mash best of all. Sweet potatoes also mash well, to serve as a savoury or sweet dish.

You can mash potatoes in several ways: using a hand masher, which gives a very smooth result; pressing the potatoes through a ricer, sieve or mouli grater, which gives a very light and fluffy result; using a fork, which can result in a slightly lumpy, uneven mixture; or using a pestle-type basher. An electric hand-held mixer can be used but don't be tempted to blend or purée them in the food processor as the end product will be a very solid, gluey mixture, ideal for turning into soup.

Making Mash

There are a number of different hand mashers available for sale but the best ones are those that have a strong but open cutting grid. Simply push down on the cooked potatoes, making sure you cover every area in the pan and you will get a smooth, yet textured result.

Press potatoes through a ricer for an easy way to prepare light and fluffy mash. For a low-calorie side dish, press the potatoes straight into a heated bowl.

Alternatively beat in a generous knob of butter, some creamy milk and seasoning to taste, then continue mashing until you have a creamy, fluffy mixture.

Quick Mash Toppings

There are many simple ways to make mashed potatoes look more exciting and even tempt youngsters to try something new and unusual.

Rough up the topping on a shepherd's pie by running a fork through it.

An alternative decorative effect can be created using the back of a spoon to gently swirl the potato into soft hollows and peaks.

For a more chunky topping, use two matching spoons to make scoops or quenelle shapes, carefully moulding the potato around the sides of the spoons.

A quick and easy pattern to achieve is a lattice design. Run with a fork up and down the pie topping, before brushing with egg and then placing under a pre-heated grill to brown.

Piping Mashed Potatoes

Smooth and creamy mashed potatoes will pipe beautifully, and your results can look professional with very little practice. But it does have to be really smooth mash, since any lumps will ruin your efforts and may clog up the piping bag and nozzle. Place a large, star nozzle in a large clean piping bag and using a spoon fill the bag two-thirds with mash. Use your left hand to hold and guide the nozzle and your right hand to squeeze the potato down the bag. Practise a few times on a board, doing it slowly at first.

Duchesse Potatoes and Rosettes

These are the fancy portions which are often served in hotels. Rosettes are piped on to baking trays, brushed with beaten egg and baked until just golden to serve as a vegetable accompaniment to a main meal. They are very easy to make at home, however, if you want to impress your friends at a dinner party. You will need to use a firmer mashed potato than normal. To do this simply add egg yolks instead of milk to the potatoes in the pan and combine well. Brush with an egg glaze: 1 small egg, beaten with 15–30ml/1–2 tbsp water will give a thin mixture. Bake at 190°C/375°F/Gas 5 until golden brown.

1 Place a large, clean piping bag, fitted with a star nozzle, in a jug to hold it steady. Spoon in the thickened mashed potato until the bag is two-thirds full.

2 Start by squeezing out a small circle of potato, moving the nozzle slowly in one direction.

3 Then, still squeezing gently, fill in the centre and lift the bag up to make a cone shape.

Piped Topping

1 The same shape as above, made with a smaller nozzle, can be used to give a pie a very professional topping.

2 Bake the topping in the oven, preheated to 190°C/375°F/Gas 5 for 10-15 minutes, or grill for 5 minutes.

Potato Nests

These make a great meal for young children or an attractive dish for dinner. Fill with asparagus spears, fresh peas, sweetcorn, baked beans, soft cheese, chicken, fish or mushrooms in a creamy sauce and heat through.

1 Using the same nozzle as for duchesse potatoes pipe a large circle, or oval, on to a baking sheet or on to greaseproof paper.

2 Then fill in the base and pipe over the outer circle again to give height to the sides. Glaze and bake as for duchesse potatoes.

Piped Edgings

Many dishes can have piped potato edges. Most well known is the individual starter Coquilles St Jacques, where the potato holds the fish and creamy sauce safely in the scallop shell.

Pipe a circle, just like the potato nests, but around the edge of a cleaned scallop shell or a china version of this. Brush with egg, fill with fish mixture and then grill until golden.

Mash Flavours

To make a Mediterranean version beat in salt, pepper and good quality olive oil to give a smooth soft mixture. Serve sprinkled with plenty of finely grated Parmesan cheese.

To make a wickedly rich mash, add thick cream or crème fraîche and grated fresh nutmeg. Mix thoroughly and serve with more grated nutmeg.

To make a lovely creamy mixture, beat in good, preferably extra virgin olive oil, and enough hot milk to make a smooth, thick purée. Then flavour to taste with salt and ground black pepper and stir in a few fresh basil leaves or parsley sprigs, chopped.

Chopped, cooked cabbage, spring onions and leeks are all regional favourites which add lots of flavour to a family supper dish.

Try a spicy mixture of chilli powder, or very finely chopped chilli and chives to sprinkle over a creamy mash.

To make a crunchy texture, place a few bacon rashers under a hot grill and once they are nice and crispy, chop them up and sprinkle over the potato.

To make a nutty mash, try toasted, flaked almonds or roughly chopped nuts of your choice.

USING COOKED POTATOES

Potatoes are one of the most versatile leftovers to have in the fridge, so it is well worth cooking extra when you make them, especially if a member of the family cannot tolerate wheat or cereals. You can use mashed potatoes in fish cakes, to thicken soups or stews, to make breads and scones and for a very light pastry to use in traditional savoury dishes or quiches. Grated, cooked potato can be used for rösti, hashes, omelettes, tortillas, and even to beef up a salad.

Potato Pastry

1 Rub 100g/4oz/8 tbsp dripping, lard or butter into 450g/1lb/4 cups sifted plain flour and add 450g/1lb mashed potatoes, 10ml/2 tsp salt, 1 beaten egg and sufficient milk so that when you draw the mixture together it is smooth but firm. Chill the pastry in the fridge for 10 minutes before use.

2 Roll the pastry out on a floured surface to an even thickness and use to line a suitable dish or tin. Chill the pastry in the dish again for 1 hour before pricking the bottom and filling as wished.

Potato Croquettes

1 Enrich a firm mash with egg, as for duchesse potatoes, season or add flavourings to taste, then shape into small cylinders, rolling out with a little flour or cornflour to prevent sticking.

2 Brush lightly with beaten egg, then coat or dip into any favourite mixture, like nibbed or flaked almonds or grated cheese mixed with breadcrumbs.

3 Shallow fry in butter and oil, turning occasionally until golden brown and warmed through. Croquettes can also be deep fried, or baked until golden brown. (Try putting a nugget of cheese in the middle before cooking for a delicious starter or supper dish.)

Rösti

1 Grate cold, par-cooked, waxy potatoes, on the largest side of a grater into a bowl and season to taste.

2 Heat a mixture of butter and oil in a heavy-based non-stick pan and, when bubbling, put in spoonfuls of the grated potato and flatten down neatly. Cook over low to medium heat until the rösti are golden and crisp underneath, which takes about 7–10 minutes.

3 Turn each of the rösti over with a fish slice, taking care that they do not fall apart and continue cooking for another 5 minutes or until really crisp.

4 To prepare one large rösti, spoon the potato mixture into the bubbling fat, flatten out evenly and leave to cook over a medium heat for about 10 minutes or until turning golden underneath. To turn the rösti over easily invert it on to a large plate – use a plate that fits right into the pan over the potato.

5 Turn the pan and plate over carefully so that the rösti slips on to the plate without breaking up.

6 Gently slide it back into the pan, with an extra knob of butter if necessary. Continue cooking for another 10 minutes or until crisp underneath. Serve cut into generous slices.

BUYING AND STORING

Now that there is such a variety of potatoes to choose from, suited for every kind of cooking, it is important to think about how you plan to use your potatoes before you shop for them. Being tempted by some lovely little creamy International Kidneys or pale Pink Fir Apple potatoes, when what you want to make is a velvety thick soup or the topping for a shepherd's pie, won't give you complete success. Look at the Potato Index so that next time you go shopping you can choose the right varieties of potatoes to suit your menu ideas. If you always like to eat the skins and are concerned about what may be sprayed on them, then you would be well-advised to buy organic potatoes. Or grow your own – a very easy and rewarding task if you have the space.

When buying new potatoes check that they are really young and fresh by scraping the skin, which should peel off easily. New potatoes have a high vitamin C content so buy and eat them as fresh as possible for maximum goodness.

Maincrop potatoes should be firm. Avoid any which are soft, flabby, sprouting or have a white dusty mould.

Check for any green patches. These are a sign that the potatoes have been stored in the light and, although the rest of the potato is fine to eat, you do need to cut out these poisonous patches.

STORING

Potatoes have come from the dark and like to stay in the dark, and they do not keep too well unless carefully stored. In the warmth of a centrally heated kitchen they can start sprouting; the dampness of a cold fridge will make them sweaty and mouldy, and in too much light they begin to lose their nutritional value and start turning green. New potatoes in particular should be eaten within two or three days, to prevent mould forming on the surface. Unless they can be kept in the dark, it is better to buy in small quantities, a few pounds at a time, so that they are used quickly.

If you prefer to buy your potatoes in bulk, by the sack or in a large paper bag, then you need to find a dark, dry larder or garage, where they won't freeze in cold weather but the temperature is low enough not to encourage the growth of any sprouts.

If you are storing your potatoes in the house, put them into an open storage rack or basket or a well aerated bin in a dry, dark room.

When you buy potatoes in plastic bags remove them from the bags immediately you get them. Then store them in a suitable place.

Read the storage and keeping times of pre-packed potatoes, since these come in many varieties. Some are ready to cook, and others are already peeled or cleaned. You can even buy potatoes with seasonings or flavoured butter nowadays, but these are best consumed soon after purchasing, again read the packet for correct storage times.

PLANNING AHEAD

If you like to be organised and peel potatoes in advance – don't. Storing peeled potatoes in water will remove almost every trace of vitamin C. Even storing them tightly covered but without water in the fridge will result in nasty black potatoes.

A much better option is to almost fully cook the potatoes in their skins, leaving them very firm. They can be refrigerated like this, covered, for 2–3 days. Then when you come to use them, peel and chop the potatoes and reheat in the microwave or cook for a further 3–5 minutes with mint, or use as you would normally in a recipe. You should also find that they have far more flavour.

You can store already mashed potato covered with cling-film ready to make into rissoles or toppings.

FREEZING POTATOES

Raw potato does not freeze at all well as it goes mushy, but cooked potato freezes quite well, although it has a tendency to go watery, so make sure it is very well dried before freezing.

Pipe duchesse potatoes or rosettes on to a baking tray, freeze until hard and store in a container. Cook from frozen.

Croquettes, rissoles, potato cakes and rösti should be individually wrapped or separated by greaseproof paper and then packed in fours or eights. Partly defrost them if they contain any meat or fish, then cook as for the original recipe.

Chips can be cooked but not browned, ready for a last minute really hot fry to crisp them. Freeze them on trays and then transfer to bags. Partly defrost on kitchen paper to remove any particles of ice before deep frying in small batches.

POTATO PRODUCTS

There are many forms of prepared potato available in the shops today. Instant mashed potato, in powder or flake form, is very easy to use and now comes with popular flavour additions; potato flour makes a healthy alternative to wheat, and canned new potatoes mean a salad is made in seconds. Foil pouches contain ready-to-fry potato suppers with a very long shelf life, and an array of seasonings could give your baked potatoes, slices or wedges a welcome spark of flavour.

EQUIPMENT

The right piece of equipment for the job always makes life easier and you may find that there are now gadgets available that you haven't come across. Some tools, like potato peelers, become old friends too. If you are used to using one particular style you will be loath to change. Just glancing at the selection of equipment now available, it's difficult to know where to start. If you could try out a gadget before buying it, like trying on a dress, you would have an easier time choosing the right one. This list is designed to help.

The horizontal-angled blades are fast and easy to use on large potatoes.

Peeler with brush For dirty work you could try a swivel-blade peeler with brush attached.

Thick-grip peeler Many peelers now have good, thick grips which make light work of any peeling job and are much easier on the muscles for those with arthritic problems.

Left: Peeler with brush

Twin-bladed peeler Takes a little time getting used to, but if you are preparing large quantities of big potatoes you could be grateful for this efficiency.

Coloured peeler Modern kitchen colours are now echoed in the design of kitchen equipment such as peelers, but following the trend doesn't always produce quality products. Enjoy them for what they are, a touch of fun in the kitchen, and hope that they also work well.

Above: Lancashire peelers

Peelers

Lancashire peeler This is the most traditional peeler, with a solid handle, often made from wood and string, and a rigid blade. They are firm and last well and also double up as a corer.

Stainless steel peeler Lightweight and inexpensive. The sharpest ones will give the thinnest peel. Beware the very cheap ones with stainless steel blades that bend, snap or blunt very quickly.

Above: Thick-grip peelers

Above: Stainless steel peeler

Swivel-blade peeler These are for left- or right-handed people, but they are not very strong for heavy-duty work.

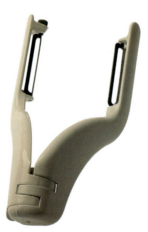

Above: Twin-bladed peeler

Above: Coloured peelers

Above: A selection of graters, including single-sided, box and standard shapes

Graters

The sturdier the better is the only approach if you want a grater for heavy-duty work, like grating large, raw potatoes. Standard or box graters are ideal and can have four or more sides with several different size blades, often including a slicer which acts like a mandoline. Some have simple removable base trays or come in their own box container, making it unnecessary to dirty a board or plate and leaving no messy trail. Single-sided graters can be difficult to hold unless you steady them with a damp cloth, but they are ideal to place over a bowl so that you can grate straight in. If you plan to put your grater in the dishwasher, look for a stainless steel one without too much plastic.

Paring Knives

These are one of the most important items in the kitchen, especially for small fiddly jobs. Choose a knife with a short enough blade to allow you to use your thumb as well, but not too short or you won't be able to use it for small chopping jobs. The knife should be curved but not serrated and it should have a sharp point. Don't be tempted by those with removable peeler blades, as these are easily lost and remove too much skin.

Above: Paring knives

Mandolines

The original mandoline was a simple wooden implement with adjustable flat or fluted blades. It was designed for chefs to cut wafer-thin slices of potato, or other hard foods like carrots, for making crisps and game chips and for shredding and chipping. Take care, as they can give your hands a nasty cut.

Modern mandolines These now often come in their own supporting plastic frame or box, sometimes with a shredder or chipper blade as well. They can have two or three blades which are adjustable to give variable thicknesses, and these are flat or fluted. Some of the plastic ones are machine washable and come with a gadget for holding the last part of the vegetable to protect you from slicing your fingertips.

For large quantities of chips and crisps where the thickness needs to be exact, a more professional mandoline is available, but it is very expensive.

Wire Baskets

Using a wire basket is the easiest way to remove a batch of chips quickly from hot fat or quantities of potato from boiling water. When putting potatoes into hot fat do be sure the basket is heated in the fat first or the potatoes will stick to it.

Left: Mandoline

Long-handled wire baskets For blanching or frying chips in, these come in various sizes. Be sure to choose one that fits your pan almost exactly.
Small baskets Used for removing small quantities or pieces of potato when blanching or frying. There is a special attached pair for making potato nests.

Steamers

Steaming gives a very light potato and has nutritional benefits since it allows far less of the vitamins to be lost during cooking. Electric steamers are excellent for large quantities of potatoes. Chinese steamer baskets, which have their own lids, are also good, especially as you can stack them up and steam several different foods at once. Clean steamers well to remove the potato starch – this is easiest done whilst they are warm.
Stainless steel steamer Can be bought with its matching pan, or separately to stand over a similar sized pan. It should

Above: Stainless steel steamer

also have a lid which makes it very useful for keeping cooked potatoes warm until needed.
Collapsible steamer These will fit into most sizes of pan. Alternatively, use a colander or sieve with your pan lid.

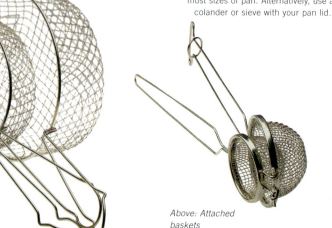

Above: Large wire baskets

Above: Attached baskets

Below: Metal ricer

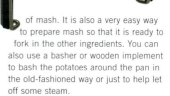

Below: Mouli grater

Ricers and Mashers

A ricer is a small rigid sieve with a pusher that makes the cooked potato come through looking like grains of rice. Potato was often served like this, riced directly into a warmed serving dish without any butter or milk added – a much healthier version

of mash. It is also a very easy way to prepare mash so that it is ready to fork in the other ingredients. You can also use a basher or wooden implement to bash the potatoes around the pan in the old-fashioned way or just to help let off some steam.

Original metal ricer This has a triangular shaped bowl and is very sturdy. The round ricer doesn't take quite so much potato in the bowl.

Plastic ricer These are machine washable. They can have two sizes of blades, for smooth or textured results.

Mashers These come in various shapes and with different size holes, so you can choose accordingly if you prefer a smooth or rough mash. Some, but not all mashers, are machine washable.

Wooden basher A strong tool, which can give a chunky or fine result.

Large mouli grater This gives a very smooth result, and is suitable for puréeing or preparing a baby's dinner.

Left: Mashers

Electrical Equipment

Food processor If you frequently slice, shred or chip potatoes then a processor with these attachments could be a great time-saver. Different models have different attachments so research well before you buy. Most will have one slicer and one shredder blade, some will have additional sizes of blades and shredders and some also have chipper attachments.

Potato peeler It only takes a few minutes to peel the potatoes, whilst you are doing other things. It does leave a slightly rough surface on the potatoes which is good for roasting, but don't put too many in the machine at one time.

Deep-fat Fryers

Chip frying is one of the greatest causes of house fires so if you are a chip-loving family, it is essential that you buy an efficient deep-fat fryer (electric or not). Check the size before you buy as some can be quite small. Cooking chips in smaller quantities gives better results, and you should never be tempted to put in too many chips as the fat may bubble over. Don't buy a cheap fryer thinking it is saving you money because it won't last as long and will probably not be as safe. For the most efficient results be sure to keep the fryer well cleaned, change the oil frequently and preferably after each use. A good non-electric deep-fat fryer should be quite heavy, with a strong heatproof handle or handles and good-fitting basket and lid.

Electric deep-fat fryers These have a thermostatically controlled temperature gauge so you fry at the right temperature, giving the crispest results. They often include specified temperature guides or controls for certain frying tasks. The fat and chips are in a sealed container which avoids smells and spitting fat and removes much of the danger. Most can be taken to pieces for easy cleaning or have removable electric cords and some have Perspex lids so that you can see the chips cooking.

Above: Deep-fat fryer

Potato Bake Stands

To speed up baking you can push your potatoes on to skewers, or stand them upright on a special potato bake stand, which can save up to one-third of the cooking time.

Above: Food processor

Above: Potato bake stand

Chip Cutters

Manual chip cutters can certainly take the time out of chip making but you will always have to cut the potato to fit the model before you start cutting chips. It really would be good if you could try these out first though, as they rely entirely on brute force. Blades should be removable for easy washing and the rest of the machine should also be easily washable.

Flat chip cutter This gives very neat, if small, chips, but is hard work.

Upright chip cutter Slightly easier to push down, this cutter has two sizes of blade but is very limited on the size of potato it can take.

Above: Scrubbing brushes

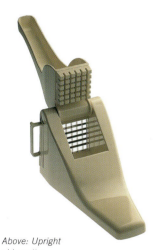

Above: Upright chip cutter

Scrubbing brushes

For easily cleaning mud off potatoes, a small brush is ideal. The bristles should be firm without being too hard on the skins as you do not want to remove then while you are scrubbing.

Potato Pots

The two terracotta and clay pots illustrated are designed specifically for potatoes, giving an earthy taste and an easy method of cooking. Remember to soak the pots in water before using, as it is this moisture which is important in the cooking.

Potato Ballers

To make potato garnishes or shapes, the large side of a potato baller is ideal if you have a firm wrist.

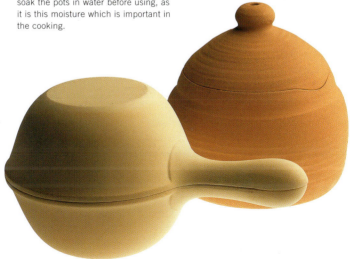

Right: Potato pots

Potatoes of the World

WITH THE REVIVAL OF OLD POTATO BREEDS and the creation of many new and unusual breeds, potatoes are fast becoming a hot fashion food. We can now choose from small, flaky new potatoes with their buttery sweet flavour; traditional maincrops with soft earthy tasting floury centres; waxy golden maincrop potatoes with velvety firm texture, small misshapen speciality potatoes which give delicious crunch to salads, omelettes and casseroles; and a growing collection of vivid red or pink, purple and blue potatoes trendy enough to grace many a London or New York restaurant menu.

This resumé includes a description of each potato along with details of origin, availability, suitability for cooking and, where relevant, for home growing. The potatoes are listed alphabetically in their most familiar name. Their seasonal details, classified according to how early in the season they are ready for digging up, are listed as: First Early, Second Early, Maincrop (early and late). This simply means that, anywhere in the world, the first earlies are the first new potatoes on the market ready for eating fresh and young, the second earlies are still theoretically a new potato although the skin will have begun to set so they will not be scrapers, whilst the maincrop potatoes which are on the market throughout most of the year are the ones that can be picked and stored for many months. However, the consumer may be even more confused by the fact that some potatoes are now being picked young for the early market as well as at full size for the maincrop market and others, which are transported from around the world, arrive labelled as new during the maincrop season! The label (if any) and the retailer may be able to help you but this index should be your best guide.

Ajax
Second Early
Origin: Netherlands
Availability: Netherlands, Pakistan, Vietnam
Suitability for cooking: Boiling, Chipping, Roasting
Description: Oval, with smooth yellow skin, pale yellow firm flesh, slightly bland in flavour

Alcmaria
First Early
Origin: Netherlands, 1970
Availability: Italy, United Kingdom
Suitability for cooking: Baking, Boiling and most other methods
Description: Long, oval, with yellow skin and firm flesh, and shallow eyes

Above: Ailsa
Above left: Alcmaria
Below: Alex

Accent
First Early
Origin: Netherlands, 1994
Availability: Netherlands, United Kingdom (not widely available yet)
Suitability for cooking: Boiling, Salad
Description: Uniform oval or round shape, light yellow smooth skin, waxy flesh which holds its shape, and bland taste. Scrapes easily and good for sautéeing
Home growing: Available

Agria
Maincrop
Origin: West Germany, 1985
Availability: Canada, New Zealand, Switzerland, United Kingdom
Suitability for cooking: Baking, Boiling, Chipping, Processing, Roasting
Description: Good size oval shape, deep yellow flesh and good flavour

Ailsa
Maincrop
Origin: Scotland, 1984
Availability: United Kingdom
Suitability for cooking: Boiling, Chipping, Processing
Description: Round or oval medium potato, white skinned with light, creamy-coloured flesh and pleasant flavour, with a floury texture
Home growing: Available

Alex
Second Early
Origin: Denmark, 1995
Availability: Europe, United Kingdom
Suitability for cooking: Salad and most other methods
Description: Splash of blue on the skin, creamy waxy texture and good mild flavour
Home growing: Good

Anna
Maincrop
Origin: Irish Republic, 1996
Availability: Irish Republic,
United Kingdom
Suitability for cooking: Baking and boiling
Description: Uniform shape with smooth
white skin and creamy while floury flesh;
often sold pre-packed

Ambo   *Above: Ambo*
Maincrop
Origin: Irish Republic, 1993
Availability: Irish Republic, New Zealand,
Switzerland, United Kingdom
Suitability for cooking: Baking, Boiling
and quite good all-round variety
Description: Creamy skin with
large pink eye patches
and very white, bland
floury flesh

Anya
Second Early
Origin: Scotland, 1997
Availability: United Kingdom
Suitability for cooking: Boiling, Salad and
speciality uses
Description: Small finger potato, knobbly
long oval shape with pale
pink beige skin, white
flesh, a waxy
texture and
pleasant
nutty
flavour

Aminca
First Early
Origin: Netherlands,
1977
Availability: Denmark,
Italy, United Kingdom
Suitability for cooking:
Baking, Boiling, Chipping
Description: Oval, medium
to large potato, with light
yellow skin and cream or
light yellow flesh, medium
deep eyes, and dry
texture. Often used for
crisp production

Above: Anya
Top right: Aminca

Arran Banner
Maincrop – early
Origin: Scotland, 1927
Availability: Cyprus, New Zealand, Portugal, United Kingdom
Suitability for cooking: Boiling
Description: Round potato with quite deep eyes and white skin and a firm, creamy flesh

Arran Comet
First early
Origin: Scotland, 1957
Availability: United Kingdom
Suitability for cooking: Boiling, Chipping
Description: Round to oval with white skin and creamy flesh. Excellent early season new potato, not quite so easily found now

Arran Consul
Maincrop – early
Origin: Scotland, 1925
Availability: United Kingdom
Suitability for cooking: Boiling, Baking, Mashing, Roasting and generally good all-round variety
Description: Round with white skin and creamy flesh. Reputed to be "the potato that helped win the war", as it provided good food for little money

Arran Victory *Irish Blues*
Maincrop – late
Origin: Scotland, 1918
Availability: United Kingdom (now rare in England and limited in Scotland and Northern Ireland)
Suitability for cooking: Baking, Boiling, Roasting and other methods
Description: Oval shape with deep purple skin and bright white flesh. This is the oldest Arran variety still available, it is a very tasty potato with a floury texture and though not easy to find it is having a revival of interest so it is well worth looking out for
Home growing: Available

Above: Arran Victory
Below from left to right: Arran Banner, Arran Comet, Arran Consul (top right)

Atlantic
Maincrop – early/mid-season
Origin: USA, 1978
Availability: Australia, Canada, New
Zealand, USA (North Carolina)
Suitability for cooking: Baking, Boiling,
Chipping, Mashing, Processing, Roasting
Description: Oval to round shape with
light, scaly, buff skin and white flesh.
Used largely for chips and crisps
Home growing: Available

Ausonia
Second Early
Origin: Netherlands, 1981
Availability: Greece, Netherlands,
United Kingdom
Suitability for cooking: Baking, Boiling
and most other methods
Description: Oval shape with white skin
and light yellow mealy flesh. It is
susceptible to discolouring after cooking.
Predominantly sold in various
pre-packed forms
Home growing: Available

Avalanche
Maincrop – early
Origin: Northern Ireland, 1989
Availability: United Kingdom (still rare)
Suitability for cooking: Boiling, Mashing

Description: Round or oval, medium
potatoes, with white skin, firm, creamy
flesh and good, slightly sweet flavour
Home growing: Available

Avondale
Maincrop
Origin: Irish Republic, 1982
Availability: Canary Isles, Egypt, Hungary,
Israel, Morocco, Pakistan, Portugal,
Spain, Sri Lanka, United Kingdom
(but still rare)
Suitability for cooking: Quite good
all-round variety
Description: Round or oval with pale,
beige skin and creamy flesh. It has a
moist waxy texture and mellow flavour

Barna
Maincrop – late
Origin: Irish Republic, 1993
Availability: Irish Republic,
United Kingdom
Suitability for cooking: Boiling, Roasting
Description: Uniform, oval red-skinned
potato with white slightly waxy flesh and
warm, nutty taste
Home growing: Available

Above: Atlantic
Left: From top to bottom, Avalanche,
Avondale, Barna

Belle de Fontenay *Boulangère Henaut*
Maincrop – early
Origin: France, 1885
Availability: Australia, France,
United Kingdom (occasionally)
Suitability for cooking: Boiling,
Mashing, Salad
Description: Long, slightly bent shape
with pale yellow skin, yellow flesh, firm
and waxy with an excellent buttery
flavour. One of the old classic potatoes of
French cuisine but popular with modern
chefs. Improves with storage. Good
eaten with skins on and tossed in
salad dressings
Home growing: Good

BelRus
Maincrop – late
Origin: USA, 1978
Availability: Canada, USA (north-eastern
states and North Florida)
Suitability for cooking: Baking,
Chipping, Mashing
Description: Uniform, long smooth
potatoes with dark thick russeted skin

and creamy coloured flesh. Exceptional
cooking qualities, excellent in gratins and
when steamed; the heavy russeting gives
a thick and crunchy skin when baked

BF15
Second Early
Origin: France, 1947
Availability: France (seldom found
outside France)
Suitability for cooking: Boiling,
Salad
Description: Long, slightly bent,
with smooth yellow skin and
yellow flesh, firm and waxy
with very good flavour.
Derivative of Belle de Fontenay
but slightly earlier
Home growing: Available

Bintje
Maincrop – early
Origin: Netherlands, 1910
Availability: Australia, Brazil, Canada,
Denmark, Finland, Italy, Netherlands,
New Zealand, Sweden, Thailand,

United Kingdom
Suitability for cooking: Baking, Boiling,
Chipping, Processing, Roasting, Salad
Description: Long, oval, with pale yellow
skin and starchy flesh and a really
distinctive flavour. Used largely for chips
and processing
Home growing: Available

Above: BelRus
*Main picture: Clockwise from right,
BF15, Bishop, Bintje*

Bishop (the)
Maincrop – late
Origin: United Kingdom, 1912
Availability: United Kingdom
Suitability for cooking: Boiling,
Roasting, Salad
Description: Long, oval potatoes, with
white skins and yellow nutty-flavoured
flesh. Recently popular variety
Home growing: Available

British Queen(s)
Second Early
Origin: Scotland, 1894
Availability: United Kingdom
Suitability for cooking: Baking, Boiling,
Roasting, Processing, Salad
Description: Kidney-shaped, with smooth
white skin and very white flesh which is
dry, floury and has a very good taste.
Best cooked with skins on to retain
excellent flavour. Very popular at the turn
of the century and having a revival

CalWhite
Maincrop
Origin: USA, 1997
Availability: Canada, USA (California, Idaho)
Suitability for cooking: Baking, Chipping,
Processing
Description: Oblong shape with buff-
white smooth skin and white flesh

Cara White and Red
Maincrop – late
Origin: Irish Republic, 1976
Availability: Cyprus, Egypt, Irish
Republic, Israel, United Kingdom
Suitability for cooking: Baking, Boiling,
Chipping and all other methods,
especially wedges.
Description: Round or oval, white skin
with pink eyes, cream flesh, mild flavour
and moist, waxy texture. There is a pink-
skinned variety which has creamy flesh
Home growing: Good, but not in very
wet soil

Carlingford
First Early
Origin: Northern Ireland, 1982
Availability: Australia, United Kingdom
Suitability for cooking: Baking,
Boiling, Chipping
Description: Round or oval with white
skin and flesh, eyes shallow to medium,
firm and waxy cooked texture and
distinctive flavour. An excellent new or
baby potato. Best not overcooked, very
good steamed, microwaved and baked
in wedges. Relatively new potato but
growing in popularity
Home growing: Available

Above left: British Queen
Above right: Carlingford
Below: Cara White

Centennial Russet
Maincrop
Origin: USA, 1977
Availability: USA (California, Colorado, Idaho, Oregon, Texas, Washington)
Suitability for cooking: Baking, Boiling, Mashing
Description: Oblong to oval with thick, dark, netted skin, shallow eyes and white floury flesh

Champion
Maincrop – late
Origin: United Kingdom, 1876
Availability: No longer commercially grown, only found in collections
Suitability for cooking: Excellent all-round variety
Description: Round potato with white skin and yellow flesh on the inside. It has an excellent flavour. It was hugely successful for very many years until much of the stock was affected by blight, but remained Ireland's favourite until the 1930s

Charlotte *Noirmoutier*
Maincrop
Origin: France, 1981
Availability: France, Germany, Italy, Switzerland, United Kingdom
Suitability for cooking: Baking, Boiling, Salad
Description: Pear or long oval shape with pale yellow skin, yellow flesh, firm waxy texture and a hint of chestnut flavour. Excellent steamed and in salads. Especially popular in France
Home growing: Good

Catriona and Blue Catriona
Second Early
Origin: Scotland, 1920; Blue Catriona, United Kingdom, 1979
Availability: United Kingdom (mainly for gardeners, in few shops)
Suitability for cooking: Baking, Boiling and all other methods
Description: Large kidney-shaped potato with skin that has beautiful purple splashes around the eyes, pale yellow flesh and a very good flavour.
Home growing: Available

Above: Centennial Russet
Left: Catriona

Chieftain
Maincrop
Origin: USA, 1966
Availability: Canada, USA
Suitability for cooking: Baking, Boiling
Description: Oblong to round with a fairly smooth, bright red skin and white flesh. Good for most methods of cooking except chipping

Chipeta
Maincrop – late
Origin: USA, 1993
Availability: Canada, USA
(Colorado, Idaho)
Suitability for cooking: Baking, Boiling, Chipping, Processing
Description: Round with white skin and patches of russeting, creamy white flesh. Mainly developed for chipping

Claret
Maincrop – early
Origin: Scotland, 1996
Availability: Scotland
Suitability for cooking: Good all-round
Description: Smooth rosy red skin, with a round to oval shape and cream, firm flesh
Home growing: Good

Top: Claret, Chieftain
Above: Cleopatra, Colmo

Cleopatra
First Early
Origin: Netherlands, 1980
Availability: Algeria, Hungary
Suitability for cooking: Boiling
Description: Oval with pink/red blemished skin and light yellow, dense flesh

Colmo
First Early
Origin: Netherlands, 1973
Availability: Netherlands,
United Kingdom
Suitability for cooking: Boiling and good for all other methods
Description: Medium-round, or oval-shaped potato, with white skin and light yellow firm flesh on the inside. Good for making mashed potatoes

Congo
Maincrop – late
Origin: Congo
Availability: Australia, United Kingdom
(for curiosity and fun for gardeners, not
in shops)
Suitability for cooking: Boiling,
Mashing, Salad
Description: Striking small, thin and
knobbly shape, with very dark, purple-
black shiny skin and beetroot black
flesh. The flavour is surprisingly bland
and the texture stodgy. It is dry when
cooked but still retains its colour, making
it impressive in salads and as a garnish.
Peel after cooking and either boil briefly,
steam or microwave. Makes good
mashed potatoes or gnocchi
Home growing: Available mainly as a
curiosity. Since they are small and dark,
you might need to harvest them on a
bright day

Above right: Désirée
Below: Congo

Delcora
Maincrop – early
Origin: Netherlands, 1988
Availability:
Netherlands, New
Zealand
Suitability for cooking:
Boiling, Chipping,
Mashing
Description: Long oval
potato with pink/red
skin and light
yellow flesh
which is not
floury and
has good
flavour

Désirée
Maincrop
Origin: Netherlands, 1962
Availability: Algeria, America, Argentina,
Australia, Cameroon, Chile, Iran, Irish
Republic, Malawi, Morocco, Netherlands,
New Zealand, Portugal, Sri Lanka,
Pakistan, Tunisia, Turkey, United Kingdom
Suitability for cooking: Baking, Boiling,
Chipping, Mashing, Roasting, Salad and
all other methods
Description: Oval shape with shallow
eyes and smooth red skin, pale creamy
yellow flesh, firm texture and good taste.
Said to be the world's most popular red-
skinned potato. It is often sold direct
from the farm and markets in large
quantities as well as loose or pre-packed.
Good roasted or cooked as wedges or
slices; holds its shape
Home growing: Good

Diamant
Maincrop – early
Origin: Netherlands, 1982
Availability: Cameroon, Canada, Egypt,
New Zealand, Pakistan
Suitability for cooking: Baking, Boiling
Description: Long oval shape, rough
white skin with light yellow, firm, waxy
flesh and nutty, sharp aftertaste. Popular
in the 1930s

Below: Duke of York
Bottom: Clockwise from top left,
Diamant, Ditta, Dr McIntosh

Ditta
Second Early
Origin: Austria, 1950
Availability: Austria, Netherlands,
United Kingdom
Suitability for cooking: Boiling, Roasting
Description: Long, oval potato with
rough, brownish skin, pale yellow flesh
and firm waxy texture. When cooked
it has a very buttery taste, and an almost
melt-in-the-mouth flavour

Dr McIntosh
Maincrop – early
Origin: United Kingdom, 1944
Availability: New Zealand, United
Kingdom (rarely found today)
Suitability for cooking: Baking, Boiling,
quite good all-round
Description: Oval potato with quite a long
shape to it with white skin and light,
creamy flesh

Draga
Second Early
Origin: Netherlands, 1970
Availability: Iran, New Zealand
Suitability for cooking: Boiling, Mashing,
Salad, Good all-round variety
Description: Round, white/yellow skin,
creamy flesh, full-flavoured with waxy
texture. Keeps well

Duke of York *Eersteling*
First Early
Origin: Scotland, 1891
Availability: Netherlands, France,
United Kingdom
Suitability for cooking: Boiling and most
other methods
Description: Long, oval, with pale
whitish-yellow skin, light yellow flesh, firm
cooked texture and rich, sweet flavour.
Best eaten young
Home growing: Very popular

Duke of York Red *Rode Eersteling*
First Early
Origin: Netherlands, 1842
Availability: Netherlands, United
Kingdom (but quite rare)
Suitability for cooking: Boiling, Salad
Description: Long, oval, very red potato
with light yellow tasty flesh. Loses its
colour when cooked
Home growing: Available

Dunbar Standard
Maincrop – late
Origin: Scotland, 1936
Availability: United Kingdom, Ireland

Suitability for cooking: Good all-round
Description: Long, oval white-skinned
potato with white flesh. Its full flavour
and firmness suit most forms of cooking.
Home growing: Available. Does well in
heavy soil

Dundrod
First Early
Origin: Northern Ireland, 1987
Availability: Canada, Netherlands,
Northern Ireland, Sweden,
United Kingdom
Suitability for cooking: Boiling,
Chipping, Mashing
Description: Oval to round
shaped potatoes with light
yellow skin and creamy
white flesh on the
inside. Moderately
waxy, so rarely falls
apart. A very popular
choice of potato for
making chips in fish
and chip shops

Edgcote Purple
Maincrop – early
Origin: United Kingdom, 1916
Availability: Collections only
Description: Long, oval potatoes with
blue skin and light yellow flesh.
Although it was an excellent cooker it
never became popular and is no longer
commercially available

Edzell Blue
Second Early
Origin: Scotland, pre-1915
Availability: Scotland (very little
now grown)
Suitability for cooking: Boiling, Mashing
Description: Round, blue-skinned with
bright white flesh, floury and tasty. Boil
with care as it falls apart easily. Very good
steamed and in microwave recipes
Home growing: Available

Eigenheimer
Maincrop – second early
Origin: Netherlands, 1893
Availability: Netherlands, Zaire (rarely
seen elsewhere)
Suitability for cooking: Chipping
Description: Oval, white skin and yellow
flesh, great for frying and chips, a
favourite of Dutch gardeners

Top left: Duke of York Red
Top right: Edzell Blue
Left: Dunbar Standard

Estima
Second Early
Origin: Netherlands, 1973
Availability: Algeria, Northern Europe
Suitability for cooking: Baking, Boiling,
Chipping, Roasting, and most
other methods
Description: Uniform oval shape with
shallow eyes, light yellow skin and flesh,
firm moist texture and mild flavour.
Most widely grown second early and has
an exceptionally long season. Makes a
particularly good baking potato early in
the year – very popular at the moment.
One of the first to destroy the myth that
yellow potatoes could not be popular
Home growing: Good

Elvira
Origin: Unknown
Availability: Italy
Suitability for cooking: Boiling, Chipping
Description: Medium oval potato with
shallow eyes, yellow skin and creamy
yellow flesh

Epicure
First Early
Origin: United Kingdom, 1897
Availability: Canada, United Kingdom
Suitability for cooking: Baking, Boiling
Description: Round, white skin and
creamy white flesh, firm texture, but with
deep eyes and a distinctive flavour.
The traditional Ayrshire potato and still
grown extensively in Scottish gardens
Home growing: A popular and easy to
grow variety

Top left: Estima
Above right: Elvira
Right: Epicure

Fianna
Maincrop – early
Origin: Netherlands, 1987
Availability: Netherlands, New Zealand,
United Kingdom

Suitability for cooking: Baking, Chipping,
Mashing, Processing, Roasting
Description: Smooth white skin and firm
flesh, with pleasant, floury texture
Home growing: Available

Forty Fold
Maincrop – early
Origin: United Kingdom, 1893;
Russet, United Kingdom, 1919
Availability: United Kingdom (very limited)
Suitability for cooking: Quite good all-
round variety
Description: Irregular tubers with deep
eyes, white or vivid purple skin splashed
with white or russet, creamy flesh, and
good flavour. The potato was a popular
Victorian speciality which is currently
being revived
Home growing: Available

Above: Forty fold, white and russet
Left: Fianna

Francine
Maincrop
Origin: France, 1993
Availability: France, Germany,
United Kingdom
Suitability for cooking: Boiling, Salad
Description: Red skin, white/cream flesh,
soft yet waxy texture and an
earthy taste. Great for gratins and
for steaming

Frisia
Maincrop – early
Origin: Netherlands
Availability: Bulgaria, Canada, Europe,
New Zealand
Suitability for cooking: Baking, Boiling,
Roasting, Salad
Description: Oval, creamy yellow-skinned
potato with white flesh and a moist,
slightly waxy texture

Gemchip
Maincrop – late
Origin: USA, 1989
Availability: Canada, USA (Colorado, Idaho, Oregon, Washington)
Suitability for cooking: Baking, Boiling, Chipping, Processing
Description: Short and round with smooth, light tan skin and white flesh with the occasional scaly patch

Golden Wonder
Maincrop – late
Origin: United Kingdom, 1906
Availability: United Kingdom
Suitability for cooking: Boiling, Processing, Roasting
Description: Large oval potato with light yellow flesh and russet/brown skin, very floury when cooked and tasty. Creates some of the best crisps and the flavour improves with long storage.
Home growing: Good for home growing, popular in Scotland

Goldrush
Maincrop
Origin: North Dakota, 1992
Availability: Canada, USA
Suitability for cooking: Baking, Boiling, Roasting, quite good all-round
Description: A new russet type, oblong potato with light brown netted skin and very white flesh and good flavour.

Granola
Second Early – early main
Origin: West Germany, 1975
Availability: Australia, Germany, India, Indonesia, Nepal, Netherlands, Pakistan, Switzerland, Turkey, Vietnam
Suitability for cooking: Baking, Boiling, Chipping
Description: Oval with brilliant yellow skin and creamy yellow flesh

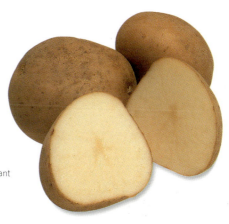

Home Guard
First Early
Origin: Scotland, 1942
Availability: United Kingdom (mainly in Cornwall and Pembrokeshire)
Suitability for cooking: Boiling, Chipping, Roasting and most other methods
Description: Round to oval, white skin and creamy white flesh, quite floury dry texture and good, almost bitter flavour. A World War II favourite, one of the first new potatoes to arrive on the market and at its best eaten early
Home growing: Good

Ilam Hardie
All year
Origin: Unknown
Availability: South Africa, New Zealand
Suitability for cooking: Baking, Boiling, Chipping, Mashing, Roasting, Salad, and most other methods
Description: Yellow skinned with white flesh, floury and well flavoured

International Kidney *Jersey Royal*
Maincrop – early
Origin: United Kingdom, 1879
Availability: Australia, Europe, United Kingdom
Suitability for cooking: Boiling, Salad
Description: Long ovals with very flaky, white/yellow skin and creamy white flesh, waxy with delicious buttery flavour. The International Kidney, developed in England in the 1870s and is slightly smaller than the original Jersey Royal. many countries have tried to grow the Jersey Royal, but only in Jersey's rich soil does this prized potato grow so well and it is now exported to many corners of the world.
Home growing: Available

Left: Francine
Above: Gemchip

Irish Cobbler *America*
First Early
Origin: USA, 1876
Availability: Canada, South Korea, USA
Suitability for cooking: Boiling, Chipping,
Mashing and most other methods.
Description: Round white, medium to
large potato, smooth creamy white skin
and flesh. Was widely grown in the
United Kingdom at the turn of the
century probably because it matures
earlier than others but has not been
grown much since World War I – except
in the USA. It is difficult to grow and
bruises easily
Home growing: Available

Itasca
Maincrop
Origin: Minnesota, 1994
Availability: Canada, USA
Suitability for cooking: Baking,
Boiling, Chipping, Mashing,
Roasting
Description: Oblong to round
shaped potato with smooth, pale
skin and creamy white flesh

Jaerla
First Early
Origin: Netherlands, 1969
Availability: Algeria, Argentina,
Greece, Netherlands, Turkey,
Yugoslavia
Suitability for cooking: Baking, Boiling

and most other methods
Description: Long, oval light skinned with
light yellow flesh and firm texture

Kanona
Maincrop
Origin: USA, 1989
Availability: Canada, USA
Suitability for cooking: Baking, Boiling,
Chipping, Processing
Description: Large round potatoes with a
white slightly netted skin and white flesh

Karlena
Origin: E. Germany, 1993
Availability: Egypt, France, Germany,
Hungary, Israel, Scandinavia, United
Kingdom (still very limited)
Suitability for cooking: Baking, Chipping,
Mashing, Roasting
Description: A medium size round
yellow skinned potato with golden yellow
flesh and warm distinctive flavour but
very floury. It is excellent as a very early
season boiling potato; main season it is
good steamed in skins, roasts and chips
very well, but boil with care to avoid
disintegration

Katahdin
Maincrop – late
Origin: USA, 1932
Availability: Canada, New Zealand, USA
Suitability for cooking: Baking, Boiling,
Salad, and most other methods
Description: Round to oblong shape, with
buff, smooth, thin skin and white, waxy,
moist flesh. Most popular in Maine
until recently

Above: Irish Cobbler
Below: Katahdin

Kennebec
Maincrop
Origin: USA, 1948
Availability: Argentina, Australia, Canada, Italy, New Zealand, Portugal, South Korea, Taiwan, Uruguay, USA
Suitability for cooking: Baking, Boiling, Chipping, Mashing, Roasting, Processing and most other methods

Description: Largish oval to round shaped potato, with smooth, buff, white skin and white flesh. Widely grown in many parts of the world now as it is adaptable and consistent. Was mainly used for chip processing but less so now although still a good all-round potato. A favourite variety for gardeners in North America

Kepplestone Kidney
Second Early – early main
Origin: United Kingdom, 1919
Availability: Not commercially available
Suitability for cooking: Boiling
Description: Blue skinned, classically shaped potatoes with yellow flesh and rich buttery taste
Home growing: Good

Kerr's Pink
Maincrop – late
Origin: Scotland, 1917
Availability: Irish Republic, Netherlands, United Kingdom
Suitability for cooking: Baking, Boiling, Chipping, Mashing, Roasting
Description: Round, pink skin, creamy white flesh, quite deep eyes, mealy, floury cooked texture
Home growing: Available

*Above: From left to right, Kennebec, Kepplestone Kidney, Karlena
Below: Kerr's Pink*

King Edward and Red
Maincrop
Origin: United Kingdom, 1902
(red 1916)
Availability: Australia, Canary Isles, New
Zealand, Portugal, Spain,
United Kingdom
Suitability for cooking: Baking,
Chipping, Mashing, Roasting and
most other methods
Description: Oval to kidney shape. White
skin with pink colouration, cream to pale
yellow flesh, floury texture. For much of
the twentieth century it was the most
popular potato in Britain and has seen a
fall and rise in popularity since
Home growing: Available

Kipfler
Maincrop
Origin: Austria, 1955
Availability: Australia (rarely available)
Suitability for cooking: Baking, Boiling,
Chipping, Roasting, Salad and most
other methods
Description: Yellow flesh and skin, small
to medium size, elongated, often called
finger potato. They have a waxy texture
when cooked and a buttery, nutty taste.
Not ideal for chipping but microwaves
well and excellent in salads

Krantz
Maincrop
Origin: USA, 1985
Availability: Canada, USA
Suitability for cooking: Baking, Boiling,
Chipping, Processing
Description: Oblong with brown russet
skin and white flesh

Linzer Delikatess
Second Early
Origin: Austria, 1976
Availability: Austria, United Kingdom
(very rare)
Suitability for cooking: Boiling, Salad
Description: Small, oval- to pear-shaped
potato with a pale yellow skin and yellow
flesh. Firm and waxy texture. The flavour
is similar to Ratte, but not so distinctive.
Good cold and in most cooked dishes
where you need firmness
Home growing: Available

Lumper
Maincrop – early
Origin: Ireland, 1806
Availability: Collections only
Description: Round, oval potato with
white skin and flesh and very deep eyes
giving it a lumpy shape. Lacking in
flavour.Dating back to the Irish famine
when it was a mainstay of the potato crop
but was nearly wiped out. Its poor
cooking qualities eventually led to the
Lumper being consigned to the history
books and seed collections only

Above: King Edward
Left: Lumper

Maori Chief
Early
Origin: New Zealand
Availability: New Zealand
Suitability for cooking: Boiling, Roasting, Salad
Description: Purple/black skin, dark purple/black flesh, with a sweet new potato flavour. The very tender skin doesn't need peeling, tastes good steamed and is best eaten within ten days of harvesting. There is also a variety found in New Zealand, with a buttery yellow flesh, which has caused much debate as to which is the true original Maori Chief potato

Marfona
Second Early
Origin: Netherlands, 1975
Availability: Cyprus, Greece, Israel, Netherlands, Portugal, Turkey, United Kingdom
Suitability for cooking: Baking, Boiling, Chipping, Mashing
Description: Round oval with light beige to yellow skin and flesh, smooth waxy texture with slightly sharp taste
Home growing: Available

Maris Bard
First Early
Origin: United Kingdom, 1972
Availability: United Kingdom
Suitability for cooking: Boiling and most other methods
Description: White skin, white to cream flesh, soft yet waxy with an earthy taste. One of the most widely grown first earlies. Can disintegrate on cooking late in the season and lose its taste
Home growing: Available

Magnum Bonum
Maincrop – late
Origin: United Kingdom, 1876
Availability: Nepal, United Kingdom (collections only)
Suitability for cooking: Baking, Boiling, Mashing, Roasting
Description: Long, oval-shaped potato with white skin and dry, mealy white flesh. Has an excellent flavour. One of the early very successful potatoes which proved to be both a good grower, an excellent eater and withstood blight. The Victorians were delighted to find such a continually good cropper which eventually was used in producing other renowned potatoes, such as today's King Edward

Majestic
Maincrop – early
Origin: Scotland, 1911
Availability: Italy, United Kingdom (now only in Scotland for seed potato)
Suitability for cooking: Baking, Boiling, Mashing
Description: Large oval with white skin and soft white flesh, and a mild flavour. Was the most widely grown variety in Britain at one time but no longer suits the marketplace and is mainly grown for gardeners and prefers dry conditions
Home growing: Available

Top left: Marfona
Right: Maori Chief

Maris Peer
Second Early
Origin: United Kingdom, 1962
Availability: United Kingdom
Suitability for cooking: Boiling,
Chipping, Salad
Description: Round- to oval-shaped
potato with cream skin and flesh, eyes
shallow to medium, firm cooked texture.
Good when young to use as new potatoes
since they do not break up on cooking,
and the large later season ones bake well
either whole or in wedges
Home growing: Available

Maris Piper
Maincrop – early
Origin: United Kingdom, 1964
Availability: Portugal, United Kingdom
Suitability for cooking: Baking, Chipping,
Processing, Roasting
Description: Oval, cream skin and flesh
and pleasant floury texture and taste.
One of Britain's most popular potatoes,
especially in fish and chip shops but
breaks up easily if overcooked
Home growing: Good

Minerva
First Early
Origin: Netherlands, 1988
Availability: Netherlands
Suitability for cooking: Boiling, Chipping

Description: Oval-shaped potato with
white skin and creamy yellow flesh on
the inside. It is particularly good for
boiling since it retains a firm texture
when cooked

Mona Lisa
Second Early
Origin: Netherlands, 1982
Availability: France, Greece,
Netherlands, Portugal
Suitability for cooking: Baking, Boiling,
Chipping, Mashing, Roasting, Processing
Description: Long oval, sometimes
kidney-shaped with yellow skin and
flesh, waxy but becomes floury when
cooked. Has a good nutty flavour. Grows
quite large for a new potato but is
surprisingly versatile in cooking. Not
grown a great deal commercially yet
Home growing: Available

Mondial
Maincrop – early
Origin: Netherlands, 1987
Availability: Greece, Israel, Netherlands,
New Zealand
Suitability for cooking: Baking, Chipping,
Mashing, Roasting
Description: Long oval with yellow skin
and flesh and a slightly mealy texture
Home growing: Good in most conditions

Above: Maris Piper
*Left: Clockwise from top, Mondial, Mona
Lisa, Morene*

Monona
Maincrop – early
Origin: USA, 1964
Availability: Canada, USA (north central and north-eastern states)
Suitability for cooking: Baking, Boiling, Chipping
Description: Round or oval, with buff-white skin and white flesh. Mainly goes for chip processing

Morene
Maincrop – early
Origin: Netherlands, 1983
Availability: Netherlands, United Kingdom
Suitability for cooking: Baking, Boiling, Chipping, Processing
Description: Large, long oval potatoes with white skin and creamy coloured mealy flesh. During cooking the flesh has a tendency to break up so do not over-boil
Home growing: Available

Nadine
Second Early
Origin: Scotland, 1987
Availability: Australia, Canary Isles, New Zealand, Spain, United Kingdom
Suitability for cooking: Baking, Boiling, Mashing, Salad
Description: Creamy yellow skin and white flesh, firm, waxy texture but slightly disappointing taste.
Sometimes available as small new potatoes with soft young skins which scrub easily. The larger ones are good baked and in wedges
Home growing: Available

Navan
Maincrop – late
Origin: Irish Republic, 1987
Availability: Irish Republic, United Kingdom

Suitability for cooking: Baking, Chipping, Roasting
Description: Oval, with white-buff skin, creamy flesh and pleasant flavour. Has a firm, waxy texture
Home growing: Available

Top: Nadine
Above: Monona

Below: Nicola

Nicola

Maincrop – all year
Origin: West Germany, 1973
Availability: Australia, Austria, Cypus, Egypt, France, Germany, Israel, Morocco, New Zealand, Portugal, Switzerland, Tunisia, United Kingdom
Suitability for cooking: Baking, Boiling, Chipping, Mashing, Roasting, Salad, and most other cooking methods
Description: Oval to long oval, with smooth yellow skin and deep yellow flesh. The texture is waxy with an excellent buttery taste. Originally grown in Mediterranean countries but now the salad-style potato has become so popular that it is being grown much more widely. Ideal for all-round use as well as being particularly good in salads – also good

steamed, sautéed and sliced for dishes taking longer to cook
Home growing: Good

Nooksak

Maincrop – late
Origin: USA, 1973
Availability: Canada, New Zealand, USA
Suitability for cooking: Baking, Boiling, Processing
Description: Oblong, slightly flat potatoes with heavily russeted skin and very white flesh. Excellent keeping potato, good for baking

Norchip

Second Early
Origin: North Dakota, 1968
Availability: Canada, USA

(North Carolina, Dakota)
Suitability for cooking: Baking, Boiling, Chipping
Description: Round to oblong shape with smooth white skin and white flesh. Excellent chipping qualities

NorDonna

Maincrop
Origin: North Dakota, 1995
Availability: Canada, USA
Suitability for cooking: Baking, Boiling, Roasting, Salad
Description: Oval- to round-shaped potatoes with dark red skin, white flesh and a good flavour. Good for microwave cooking, in soups and served cold

Above: Norchip

Norland

Early
Origin: North Dakota, 1957
Availability: Canada, USA, United Kingdom
Suitability for cooking: Baking, Boiling, Mashing, Salad
Description: Oblong, slightly flat with medium-red skin and creamy flesh. Also popular and available in Europe is the Red Norland with a rich red skin and pale flesh
Home growing: Available

Norwis

Maincrop
Origin: USA, 1965
Availability: USA
Suitability for cooking: Baking, Boiling, Chipping, Processing
Description: Large ovals, slightly flat with smooth, light tan to white skin and pale, creamy, yellow flesh

Above: Norwis

Onaway
Early
Origin: USA, 1956
Availability: Canada, USA (north-eastern states and Michigan)
Suitability for cooking: Baking, Boiling
Description: Short and round with smooth, creamy white skin and flesh

Patrones
Maincrop – early
Origin: Netherlands, 1959
Availability: Australia, Indonesia, Malawi, Pakistan, Vietnam
Suitability for cooking: Baking, Boiling, Roasting, Salad
Description: Small, oval- to pear-shaped, with light golden-yellow skin and flesh and a firm waxy texture. These potatoes are great for steaming, gratins and for rösti

Penta
Second Early
Origin: Netherlands, 1983
Availability: Canada, Netherlands
Suitability for cooking: Baking, Boiling, Mashing, Roasting
Description: Round, with quite deep pink/red eyes, creamy white skin and rich, creamy flesh. A fairly new Maincrop potato which has a tendency to disintegrate on boiling. Good for steaming and microwave dishes

Top: Penta
Left: Onaway

Pentland Hawk
Maincrop – early
Origin: Scotland, 1966
Availability: United Kingdom
Suitability for cooking: Baking, Boiling, Chipping, Processing, Roasting
Description: Oval, white skin and creamy flesh, with a good flavour.
Very popular in Scotland as it cooks well. It is an excellent keeper, but has a slight tendency to discolour after cooking. At its best late in the season
Home growing: Available

Pentland Javelin
First Early
Origin: Scotland, 1968
Availability: United Kingdom
Suitability for cooking: Boiling, Salad
Description: Medium-sized oval, white skin, white flesh, soft waxy texture. It is a good new potato but also bakes and roasts well later in the season
Home growing: Good

Pentland Marble
First Early
Origin: Scotland, 1970
Availability: United Kingdom
Suitability for cooking: Boiling, Salad
Description: Round to oval, white-skinned with light yellow waxy flesh. Good small, early, waxy salad potato, unlike most of the other Pentlands and only recently reintroduced into the market
Home growing: Available

Pentland Crown
Maincrop
Origin: Scotland, 1959
Availability: United Kingdom (Scotland, but rarely seen in shops), Malawi
Suitability for cooking: Baking, Boiling, Roasting
Description: Oval to round with white skin and creamy white flesh. The first of the Pentland varieties to become popular in the Seventies, especially in eastern England but out of favour now as it doesn't have the cooking qualities required
Home growing: Available

Pentland Dell
Maincrop – early
Origin: Scotland, 1961
Availability: New Zealand, South Africa, United Kingdom
Suitability for cooking: Baking, Chipping, Processing, Roasting
Description: Medium-sized, oval potato with white skin, creamy white flesh, and a firm fairly dry texture.
It has a tendency to disintegrate during boiling but can bake well
Home growing: Available

Pentland Squire
Maincrop – early
Origin: Scotland, 1970
Availability: United Kingdom
Suitability for cooking: Baking, Mashing, Processing, Roasting
Description: Oval, white skin and creamy white flesh, very floury texture and good flavour. Very good baker and popular with fish and chip shops
Home growing: Good

Above: Clockwise from top, the Pentland collection, Hawk, Javelin, Dell, Marble, Crown, Squire

Picasso
Maincrop – early
Origin: Netherlands, 1992
Availability: Balearic Islands, CIS,
Cyprus, Egypt, Netherlands, Spain,
Portugal, United Kingdom
Suitability for cooking: Boiling, Salad
Description: Small, oval-round potato
with quite deep red eyes, pale skin, with
white waxy flesh
Home growing: Available

Pike
Maincrop
Origin: Pennsylvania, 1996
Availability: Canada/USA
Suitability for cooking: Baking, Boiling,
Chipping, Processing
Description: Medium, spherical potatoes
with quite deep eyes, buff-coloured,
slightly netted skin and creamy flesh.
Has a tendency to discolour after it has
been cooked

Pimpernel
Maincrop – early
Origin: Netherlands, 1953
Availability: Chile, Malawi, Norway, South
Africa, Zaire

Suitability for cooking:
Good all-round
Description: An
oval shaped potato
with pink to red skin
and yellowish-
coloured flesh on
the inside

Pink Eye *Southern Gold,*
Sweet Gold or Pink Gourmet
Early
Origin: United Kingdom, 1862
Availability: Australia
Suitability for cooking: Boiling, Mashing,
Salad and most other methods
Description: A small, smooth, creamy-
skinned potato, with purple/blue blush,
and creamy yellow flesh, floury texture
and a nutty taste. Although it originated
in Kent, it is now only grown in Australia
and is commonly available as a new
potato variety

Pink Fir Apple
Maincrop – late
Origin: France, 1850
Availability: Australia, France,
United Kingdom

Suitability for cooking:
Baking, Boiling, Roasting, Salad
Description: Long, knobbly, misshapen
potatoes with a pink blush on white skins
and creamy yellow flesh. Firm and waxy
with a delicious, nutty flavour. Best
cooked in skins. Having a revival now but
they have always been popular with
gardeners as they are good keepers. The
shape makes them impossible to peel
until cooked, but they are best cold in
salads and tossed in warm dressings, or
served as new potatoes
Home growing: Good for home growing,
although tubers form clusters of roots
under stem and can be prone to blight

Above: Picasso
Left: Pink Fir Apple

Pompadour
Maincrop – early
Origin: Netherlands, 1976
Availability: France
Suitability for cooking: Boiling, Salad
Description: Long, oval and regular in
shape with light yellow skin and flesh.
Also good steamed and served on their
own for a starter

Premiere
First Early
Origin: Netherlands, 1979
Availability: Bulgaria, Canada,
Netherlands, United Kingdom
Suitability for cooking: Baking, Boiling,
Chipping, Roasting
Description: Large, oval potatoes with
light yellow skin, firm yellow flesh and
good flavour. Not as waxy as many
early potatoes
Home growing: Available

Primura
First Early
Origin: Netherlands, 1963
Availability: Denmark, Italy, Netherlands
Suitability for cooking: Boiling, Chipping
Description: Oval to round, medium size,
yellow skin, light yellow flesh, shallow
eyes and firm texture

Ratte (La) *Cornichon or Asparges
or Princess*
Maincrop – early
Origin: France, 1872
Availability: Australia, Denmark, Germany,
France (has only recently begun to be
grown outside France), United Kingdom
Suitability for cooking: Boiling, Salad
Description: Long, tubular, almost
banana-shaped, not as knobbly as Pink
Fir. Has brown/yellow skin and creamy
flesh, which is firm and waxy with a
delicious nutty flavour. Very good for
eating cold, exceptionally popular in
France and growing in popularity in other
parts of the world
Home growing: Good

*Above: From top to bottom, Ratte,
Record*

Record
Maincrop – early
Origin: Netherlands, 1932
Availability: Greece, Holland, Yugoslavia,
United Kingdom (grown in Britain for
processing market)
Suitability for cooking: Baking, Chipping,
Mashing, Roasting, Processing
Description: White skin with pinkish
tinges, light yellow to yellow flesh, mealy
texture and great flavour. Versatile potato
often sold by the sack in farm shops
Home growing: Available

*Above: From left to right, Primura,
Premiere*

Red Pontiac *Dakota Chief*
Maincrop – early
Origin: USA, 1983
Availability: Algeria, Australia, Canada, Philippines, Uruguay, USA (south-eastern states), Venezuela
Suitability for cooking: Baking, Boiling, Mashing,
Roasting, Salads
Description: Round to oval potatoes with dark red, sometimes netted skin, quite deep eyes and white waxy flesh. A red-skinned variety with worldwide popularity. Good for use in microwave cooking
Home growing: Available

Red Rascal
Maincrop
Origin: Unknown
Availability: New Zealand
Suitability for cooking: Baking,
Mashing, Roasting
Description: Red-skinned and yellow-fleshed, slightly floury with good flavour

Red Rooster
Maincrop – early
Origin: Irish Republic, 1993
Availability: Irish Republic
Suitability for cooking: Baking, Boiling, Chipping, Processing, Roasting, Salad
Description: Flattish, oval potato with bright red skin and firm buttery, yellow, mild-tasting flesh. Fairly new potato not yet widely available outside Ireland
Home growing: Available

Red LaSoda
Maincrop – late
Origin: USA, 1953
Availability: Algeria, Australia, Canada, Uruguay, USA (south-eastern states), Venezuela

Suitability for cooking: Baking, Boiling, Roasting
Description: Round to oval with smooth, deep-red skin, quite deep eyes and creamy white flesh. Ideal for most cooked and baked dishes

Right: Red LaSoda
Above: Red Rooster
Left: Red Pontiac

Above: From left, Romano, Rocket, Roseval

Red Ruby
Maincrop
Origin: USA, 1994
Availability: Canada, USA
Suitability for cooking: Baking, Boiling
Description: Oblong in shape with dark red skin which has patches of russeting and bright white flesh. An attractive winter potato

Remarka
Maincrop
Origin: Netherlands, 1992
Availability: Netherlands, Portugal, Spain, United Kingdom
Suitability for cooking: Baking, Boiling, Chipping, Roasting
Description: Large oval potato with creamy white skin, pale yellow flesh and good flavour. Makes a particularly good baking potato
Home growing: Available for home growing and ideal for organic gardening as it is a very disease-resistant variety

Rocket
First Early
Origin: United Kingdom, 1987
Availability: New Zealand, United Kingdom
Suitability for cooking: Baking, Boiling, Chipping, Mashing, Roasting, Salad
Description: Uniformly round, white-skinned, white flesh, firm, waxy and well flavoured. This is one of the earliest potatoes
Home growing: Available

Romano
Maincrop – early
Origin: Netherlands, 1978
Availability: Balearic Islands, Cameroon, CIS, Hungary, Netherlands, Portugal, Spain, United Kingdom
Suitability for cooking: Baking, Boiling, Mashing, Roasting and most other methods
Description: Round to oval, red skin with creamy flesh, soft dry texture, with a pleasant, mild nutty taste. Lovely colour which tends to pale during cooking to a soft rusty beige
Home growing: Available

Roseval
Second Early – early main
Origin: France, 1950
Availability: Australia, France, Israel, New Zealand, United Kingdom
Suitability for cooking: Boiling, Salad
Description: Oval shape with dark red, almost purple skin with golden yellow flesh. Waxy texture with a really good buttery flavour. A very distinctive-looking potato which has a great flavour and is very popular in microwave cookery
Home growing: Good

Above: Remarka

Rosine
Maincrop – early
Origin: Brittany, 1972
Availability: France
Suitability for cooking: Boiling, Salad
Description: Great in steamed dishes and gratins, also in salads

Rouge (La)
Maincrop – late
Origin: USA, 1962
Availability: Canada, USA (south-eastern and eastern states)
Suitability for cooking: Boiling, Roasting
Description: Medium size, irregular flattened round/oval with smooth bright red skin, quite deep eyes and creamy white flesh. Brilliant colour which fades in storage, but an attractive winter potato. Very popular in Florida

Royal Kidney
Second Early
Origin: United Kingdom, 1899
Availability: United Kingdom (but now grown in Majorca for United Kingdom market)
Suitability for cooking: Salad
Description: Kidney-shaped, smooth white skin with pale yellow flesh and waxy texture. Good eaten cold so works particularly well in salads

Rua
Maincrop – early
Origin: New Zealand, 1960
Availability: New Zealand
Suitability for cooking: Baking, Boiling, Chipping, Mashing, Roasting, Salad and most other methods

Description: Round-shaped potato with creamy white skin and white flesh on the inside. It falls midway between being waxy and floury in texture when cooked. This potato has a really good flavour and is good for use in many dishes

Russet Burbank *Idaho Russet or Netted Gem*
Maincrop – late
Origin: USA, 1875
Availability: Australia, Canada, New Zealand, United Kingdom (for commercial use only), USA (north-west, central and mid-eastern states)
Suitability for cooking: Baking, Chipping, Mashing, Processing, Roasting
Description: Oval to long in shape, russeted skin with pale yellow to white flesh, floury and full of flavour, and turning a bright colour when cooked. The potato which made Idaho famous for potatoes and therefore is often referred to as an Idaho potato. Hugely popular in America for some time and more recently found in McDonald's fries. Most widespread potato grown in Canada

Above left: Russet Burbank
Below: Royal Kidney

Russet Century
Maincrop – late
Origin: USA, 1995
Availability: USA
Suitability for cooking: Baking, Boiling,
Mashing, Roasting
Description: Long, cylindrical and slightly
flat potatoes with pale, buff-coloured,
slightly russeted skin and creamy flesh

Russet Frontier
Second Early
Origin: USA, 1990
Availability: Canada, USA
Suitability for cooking: Baking,
Boiling, Chipping

Description: Long, oval potatoes with
light, slightly russeted skins and creamy
white flesh

Russet Lemhi
Maincrop – late
Origin: USA, 1981
Availability: USA
Suitability for cooking: Baking, Chipping
and most other methods
Description: Large oblong with a tannish-
brown netted skin and white eyes

Russet Norking
Maincrop
Origin: USA, 1977
Availability: Canada, USA
Suitability for cooking: Baking, Boiling,
Chipping
Description: Oblong-shaped potato
with medium-heavy russet skin and
creamy white flesh

Russet Norkotah
Second Early
Origin: North Dakota, 1987
Availability: Canada, USA
Suitability for cooking: Baking, Chipping
Description: Oval long, darkly russeted
potatoes with white flesh

Russet Nugget
Maincrop – late
Origin: Colorado, 1989
Availability: Canada, USA
Suitability for cooking: Baking, Boiling,
Chipping, Processing, Roasting
Description: Oblong, slightly flat potatoes
with evenly russeted skin and creamy
white flesh

Russet Ranger
Maincrop – late
Origin: USA, 1991
Availability: Canada, USA (Colorado,
Idaho, Oregon, Washington)
Suitability for cooking: Baking, Boiling,
Chipping, Processing
Description: Long, russet or tannish-
skinned potatoes, with bright white flesh

Samba
Maincrop – early
Origin: France, 1989
Availability: France, Portugal, Spain
Suitability for cooking: Baking, Boiling,
Mashing and most other methods
Description: Regular, oval shape, white
skin with yellow flesh and floury texture
when cooked

*Above: From top, Russet Frontier,
Russet Burbank*

Sangre

Maincrop
Origin: Colorado, 1982
Availability: Canada, USA (western states)
Suitability for cooking: Baking, Boiling
Description: Oval shape with smooth dark red skin, slightly netted, and creamy flesh

Sante

Maincrop – early
Origin: Netherlands, 1983
Availability: Bulgaria, Canada, Netherlands, United Kingdom
Suitability for cooking: Baking, Boiling, Chipping, Roasting
Description: Oval or round with white or light yellow skin and flesh and dry firm texture. These have become the most successful organic potato and are often sold young as new potatoes too
Home growing: Available

Saxon

Second Early
Origin: United Kingdom, 1992
Availability: United Kingdom (still rare)
Suitability for cooking: Baking, Boiling, Chipping
Description: This variety has white skin and flesh, a firm moist texture and excellent flavour. New general purpose potato which is still finding its niche and is very popular in the pre-packed potato market
Home growing: Available

Sebago

Maincrop – late
Origin: USA, 1938
Availability: Australia, Canada, Malaysia, New Zealand, South Africa, USA (Northern states), Venezuela
Suitability for cooking: Baking, Boiling, Chipping, Mashing, Roasting, Salad
Description: Round to oval shape, with ivory white skin and white flesh. Especially good for both boiling and mashing. Most widely grown potato in Australia

Above: From left to right, Sante, Saxon (bottom), Sebago

Above: Sangre

Above: Sebago

Sharpe's Express

First – Second Early
Origin: United Kingdom, 1900
Availability: Not for commercial markets though occasionally available in Scotland
Suitability for cooking: Quite good all-round
Description: Oval to pear shaped, with white skin and creamy flesh. Needs careful cooking, especially when boiling
Home growing: Occasionally available for home growing

Shepody

Maincrop – early
Origin: New Brunswick, Canada, 1980
Availability: Canada, New Zealand, USA (Northern states)
Suitability for cooking: Baking, Boiling, Chipping, Mashing
Description: Long, oval shape, with white, slightly netted skin, light creamy yellow flesh and dry starchy texture. Developed for the chip processing market in America and seldom found in supermarkets

Shetland Black *Black Kidney*

Second Early
Origin: United Kingdom, 1923
Availability: United Kingdom (very limited)
Suitability for cooking: Boiling, Mashing
Description: Inky blue/black skin with yellow flesh and unique purple ring inside. Very fluffy and floury with an exceptionally sweet, buttery flavour. An attractive potato which, if handled carefully, can be great in salads or served simply with butter. Also good mashed, but the colour goes slightly grey/blue
Home growing: Available

Top: Shepody
Left: From top to bottom, Skerry Blue, Swedish Black, Shetland Black

Shula
Maincrop – early
Origin: United Kingdom, 1986
Availability: Scotland, but still rare
Suitability for cooking: Boiling, Mashing, Roasting, quite good all round
Description: Oval shape, partly pink skin, with light creamy flesh
Home growing: Occasionally available

Sieglinde
Second Early
Origin: West Germany, 1935
Availability: Cyprus, Germany
Suitability for cooking: Boiling, Roasting
Description: Long, oval

shape, with white skin and yellow flesh. Beware of overcooking as they tend to break up easily

Skerry Blue
Maincrop – late
Origin: United Kingdom, *c.*1846
Availability: United Kingdom (not commercially available)
Suitability for cooking: Boiling
Description: Rich violet skin with deep purple and white mottled or creamy flesh. Has a superb flavour
Home growing:
Available

Snowden
Maincrop – all year
Origin: USA, 1990
Availability: Canada, USA
Suitability for cooking: Baking, Boiling, Chipping, Processing
Description: Round, slightly flat potato with mildly netted, light tan skin and creamy flesh. Primarily used in Canada for the chip processing market

Spunta
Second Early
Origin: Netherlands, 1968
Availability: Argentina, Australia, Cyprus, Greece, Indonesia, Italy, Malaysia, Mauritius, Netherlands, New Zealand, Portugal, Thailand, Tunisia, United Kingdom, Vietnam
Suitability for cooking: Baking, Boiling, Chipping, Mashing, Roasting, Salad and most other methods
Description: Medium-large, long potato, often kidney- or pear-shaped, with light yellow skin and golden flesh
Home growing: Occasionally available

Top: Spunta
Above: Snowden

Stroma
Second Early
Origin: Scotland, 1989
Availability: New Zealand, United
Kingdom (still rare)
Suitability for cooking: Baking, Boiling,
Mashing, Roasting
Description: Attractive long, oval
potato with pink/red skin, yellow/pink
flesh, floury texture and good flavour
Home growing: Available

Superior
Second Early
Origin: USA, 1962
Availability: Canada, South Korea,
USA (North Carolina)
Suitability for cooking: Chipping and
most other methods
Description: Round to oblong,
irregular shape with buff skin,
occasionally slightly russeted or netted,
and white flesh. Best early in the season

Swedish Black
Origin: Unknown
Availability: Collections only
Suitability for cooking: Baking,
Boiling, Mashing
Description: Bluish-purple skinned
medium to large potato with very deep
eyes giving irregular shape. Blue flesh is
very mealy on cooking

Sweet Potato
Maincrop
Origin: South America
Availability: Widely grown in southern
United States and Pacific Islands,
Japan, Soviet Union
Suitability for cooking: Baking,
Boiling, Mashing, Processing,
Roasting and most other
methods
Description: Two
varieties, white skinned
and red-brown
skinned, both with
yellow flesh and quite
a waxy texture. The redder
are sweeter and firmer.
The sweet potato is
unrelated to the white potato
or to the yam. However it has all
the same characteristics: the
edible part is the tuber which can vary in
skin and flesh colour and can be treated
just like the potato. It is a staple food in

the West Indies, Africa and Asia and
has seen a rise in popularity in
Western cuisine

Above: Superior

Toolangi Delight
Origin: Australia
Availability: Australia (still new, so rarely
available yet)
Suitability for cooking: Baking, Boiling,
Chipping, Mashing, Roasting, Salad and
good all-round variety
Description: A truly distinctive purple
skin and pure smooth white flesh which
is dry when cooked. It is one of the few
potatoes bred in Australia where it is
often used to make gnocchi

Above: Sweet Potato

Up to Date
Maincrop – late
Origin: Scotland, 1894
Availability: Burma, Cyprus, Malawi,
Mauritius, Nepal, South Africa,
United Kingdom
Suitability for cooking: Quite good all-round variety
Description: Flattish oval shape, white skin and flesh with a good flavour.
First potato to be grown in Cyprus for export and still mainly grown for small international markets. It was the main variety available at the turn of the century in the United Kingdom

Valor
Maincrop – early
Origin: Scotland, 1993
Availability: Canary Isles, Israel,
United Kingdom
Suitability for cooking: Baking, Boiling
Description: Oval potato with white skin and creamy white flesh. A new potato not yet widely available in the shops
Home growing: Available

Tosca
Maincrop – late
Origin: United Kingdom, 1987
Availability: United Kingdom (still rare)
Suitability for cooking: Good
all-round variety
Description: Oval-shaped potato with pink to red skin and light yellow pleasant tasting flesh

Ulster Prince
First Early
Origin: United Kingdom, 1947
Availability: Irish Republic, United
Kingdom (very small quantities)
Suitability for cooking: Baking, Boiling,
Chipping, Roasting
Description: Large, kidney-shaped potato with white skin and white flesh. This potato is best eaten early in the season when the flavour is delicious
Home growing: Available

Ulster Sceptre
First Early
Origin: Northern Ireland, 1963
Availability: Northern Ireland

Suitability for cooking: Boiling, Roasting, Salad and most other methods
Description: Smaller ovals, with yellow-white skin and creamy waxy firm flesh. Sometimes blackening can occur after cooking which has seen it gradually being edged out of the market place

Top left: Tosca
Left: Ulster Prince (top), Ulster Sceptre
Above: Up to Date

White Rose *American Giant, Wisconsin Pride, California Long White*
First Early
Origin: USA, 1893
Availability: Canada, USA (California, Oregon, Washington)
Suitability for cooking: Baking, Boiling, Mashing
Description: Large, very long and flat with smooth white skin and quite deep eyes, and bright white flesh. Not as popular as it used to be

Wilja
Second Early
Origin: Netherlands, 1967
Availability: Netherlands, Pakistan
Suitability for cooking: Boiling, Chipping, Mashing, Roasting
Description: Long, oval shape with pale yellow skin and flesh, quite firm, with a slightly dry texture. Second most widely grown of the second-early potatoes. Often available in maincrop season
Home growing: Available

Vanessa
First Early
Origin: Netherlands, 1973
Availability: Netherlands, United Kingdom
Suitability for cooking: Boiling, Roasting, Salad
Description: Long oval with pink to red skin and light yellow flesh
Home growing: Available

Viking
Maincrop
Origin: North Dakota, USA, 1963
Availability: Canada, USA
Suitability for cooking: Baking, Boiling, Mashing and most other methods
Description: Ranging from large oblong to round with smooth, pale red skin and very white flesh

Vitelotte *Truffe de Chine*
Origin: Unknown
Availability: France, United Kingdom (very rare)
Suitability for cooking: Boiling, Salad
Description: Long, thin and smallish purple/black finger potatoes with dark greyish blue flesh. Firm waxy texture with a mild nutty taste. The colour does not fade on cooking. The name Truffe de Chine is not often used in France since there is also a Chinese Truffle (Truffe de Chine) found which causes confusion

Top right: Wilja
Above: Vitelotte
Right: White Rose

Winston
First Early
Origin: Scotland, 1992
Availability: New Zealand,
United Kingdom
Suitability for cooking: Baking, Chipping,
Roasting, Salad
Description: A uniform, oval-shaped
potato with almost no eyes, creamy white
skin and very firm texture. These
potatoes make particularly good early
season bakers
Home growing: Available

Right: Winston
Below: Yukon Gold

Yukon Gold
Second Early – Maincrop
Origin: Ontario, Canada, 1980
Availability: Canada, USA
(California, Michigan)
Suitability for cooking: Baking,
Boiling, Chipping
Description: Large, oval to round potato
with buff-coloured skin, yellow flesh, pink
eyes and a slightly mealy texture. An
excellent baking potato with a delicious
flavour, which is very popular in the
international speciality market. This was
the first successful North American
yellow-fleshed potato
Home growing: Available

The Recipes

NEW POTATOES

The new potato heralds the beginning of the potato year. We call them new or early potatoes as they are the first of that year's crop to be harvested. After as little as only 100 days underground certain potato varieties are ready for picking, their skins still fragile and flaky and their flesh firm and often quite crisp when lightly cooked.

The best new potatoes are quite delicious simply served with butter and fresh herbs, but to the creative cook they are surprisingly flexible. When still quite firm, almost crunchy, they are great in salads and their fresh earthy tastes can cope with the strong tangy flavours of Toulouse or Cajun salads. Firm, waxy new potatoes are ideal to skewer and barbecue, or try serving them with the melted Swiss cheese, raclette. And as they get bigger, towards the end of the new season, they are great thickly sliced for casseroles and pies, perfect for roasting whole with onions and herbs, and ideal layered into frittatas. Waxy potatoes are also delicious in the Italian classic dish, Gnocchi.

TANGY POTATO SALAD

IF YOU LIKE A GOOD KICK OF MUSTARD, YOU'LL LOVE THIS COMBINATION. IT'S ALSO WELL FLAVOURED WITH TARRAGON, USED IN THE DRESSING AND AS A GARNISH.

SERVES EIGHT

INGREDIENTS

   1.55kg/3lb small new or salad
     potatoes
   30ml/2 tbsp white wine vinegar
   15ml/1 tbsp Dijon mustard
   45ml/3 tbsp vegetable or olive oil
   75g/3oz/6 tbsp chopped red onion
   125ml/4fl oz/½ cup mayonnaise
   30ml/2 tbsp chopped fresh tarragon,
     or 7.5ml/1½ tsp dried tarragon
   1 celery stick, thinly sliced
   salt and ground black pepper
   celery leaves, to garnish
   tarragon leaves, to garnish

VARIATIONS
When available, use small red or even blue potatoes to give a nice colour to the salad.

1 Cook the potatoes in their skins in boiling salted water for about 15–20 minutes until tender. Drain well.

2 Mix together the vinegar and mustard, then slowly whisk in the oil.

3 When the potatoes are cool enough to handle, slice them into a large bowl.

4 Add the onion to the potatoes and pour the dressing over them. Season, then toss gently to combine. Leave to stand for at least 30 minutes.

5 Mix together the mayonnaise and tarragon. Gently stir into the potatoes, along with the celery. Serve garnished with celery leaves and tarragon.

TOULOUSE POTATO SALAD

WELL-FLAVOURED SAUSAGES AND FIRM CHUNKY POTATOES MAKE A REALLY GREAT LUNCH, SIMPLY DRESSED WITH A QUICK AND EASY VINAIGRETTE.

3 Peel the potatoes if you like or leave in their skins, and cut into 5mm/¼in slices. Place them in a large bowl and sprinkle with the wine and shallots.

4 To make the vinaigrette, mix together the mustard and vinegar in a small bowl, then very slowly whisk in the oil. Season and pour over the potatoes.

SERVES FOUR

INGREDIENTS
    450g/1lb small waxy or
      salad potatoes
    30–45ml/2–3 tbsp dry white wine
    2 shallots, finely chopped
    15ml/1 tbsp chopped fresh parsley
    15ml/1 tbsp chopped fresh tarragon
    175g/6oz cooked garlic or
      Toulouse sausage
    chopped fresh parsley, to garnish
For the vinaigrette
    10ml/2 tsp Dijon mustard
    15ml/1 tbsp tarragon vinegar or
      white wine vinegar
    75ml/5 tbsp extra virgin olive oil
    salt and ground black pepper

1 Cook the potatoes in their skins in a large saucepan of boiling salted water for 10–12 minutes until tender.

2 Drain the potatoes, rinse under cold running water, then drain them again.

5 Add the chopped herbs to the potatoes and toss until well mixed.

6 Slice the sausage and toss with the potatoes. Season to taste and serve at room temperature with a parsley garnish.

HOT HOT CAJUN POTATO SALAD

IN CAJUN COUNTRY WHERE TABASCO ORIGINATES, HOT MEANS REALLY HOT, SO YOU CAN GO TO TOWN WITH THIS SALAD IF YOU THINK YOU CAN TAKE IT!

SERVES SIX TO EIGHT

INGREDIENTS

    8 waxy potatoes
    1 green pepper, seeded and diced
    1 large gherkin, chopped
    4 spring onions, shredded
    3 hard-boiled eggs, shelled
     and chopped
    250ml/8fl oz/1 cup mayonnaise
    15ml/1 tbsp Dijon mustard
    salt and ground black pepper
    Tabasco sauce, to taste
    pinch or two of cayenne
    sliced gherkin, to garnish
    mayonnaise, to serve

1 Cook the potatoes in their skins in boiling salted water until tender. Drain and leave to cool. When they are cool enough to handle, peel them and cut into coarse chunks.

2 Place the potatoes in a large bowl and add the green pepper, gherkin, spring onions and hard-boiled eggs. Toss gently to combine.

3 In a separate bowl, mix the mayonnaise with the mustard and season with salt, black pepper and Tabasco sauce to taste.

4 Toss the dressing into the potato mixture and sprinkle with a pinch or two of cayenne. Serve with mayonnaise and a garnish of sliced gherkin.

POTATO GNOCCHI

GNOCCHI ARE LITTLE ITALIAN DUMPLINGS MADE EITHER WITH MASHED POTATO AND FLOUR, OR WITH SEMOLINA. TO ENSURE THAT THEY ARE LIGHT AND FLUFFY, TAKE CARE NOT TO OVERMIX THE DOUGH.

4 Divide the dough into 4 pieces. On a lightly floured surface, form each into a roll about 2cm/¾in in diameter. Cut the rolls crossways into pieces about 2cm/¾in long.

5 Hold an ordinary table fork with tines sideways, leaning on the board. Then one by one, press and roll the gnocchi lightly along the tines of the fork towards the points, making ridges on one side, and a depression from your thumb on the other.

SERVES FOUR TO SIX

INGREDIENTS

1kg/2¼lb waxy potatoes
250–300g/9–11oz/2¼–2¾ cups
  plain flour, plus more
  if necessary
1 egg
pinch of freshly grated nutmeg
25g/1oz/2 tbsp butter
salt
fresh basil leaves, to garnish
Parmesan cheese cut in shavings,
  to garnish

COOK'S TIP
Gnocchi are also excellent served with a heated sauce, such as Bolognese.

1 Cook the potatoes in their skins in a large saucepan of boiling salted water until tender but not falling apart. Drain and peel while the potatoes are still hot.

2 Spread a layer of flour on a work surface. Pass the hot potatoes through a food mill, dropping them directly on to the flour. Sprinkle with about half of the remaining flour and mix in very lightly. Break the egg into the mixture.

3 Finally add the nutmeg to the dough and knead lightly, adding more flour if the mixture is too loose. When the dough is light to the touch and no longer moist it is ready to be rolled.

6 Bring a large pan of salted water to a fast boil, then drop in about half the prepared gnocchi.

7 When the gnocchi rise to the surface, after 3–4 minutes, they are done. Lift them out with a slotted spoon, drain well, and place in a warmed serving bowl. Dot with butter. Cover to keep warm while cooking the remainder. As soon as they are cooked, toss the gnocchi with the butter, garnish with Parmesan shavings and fresh basil leaves, and serve at once.

POTATOES, PEPPERS AND SHALLOTS ROASTED WITH ROSEMARY

THESE POTATOES SOAK UP BOTH THE TASTE AND WONDERFUL AROMAS OF THE SHALLOTS AND ROSEMARY — JUST WAIT TILL YOU OPEN THE OVEN DOOR.

SERVES FOUR

INGREDIENTS
    500g/1¼lb waxy potatoes
    12 shallots
    2 sweet yellow peppers
    olive oil
    2 rosemary sprigs
    salt and ground black pepper
    crushed peppercorns, to garnish

1 Preheat the oven to 200°C/400°F/Gas 6. Par-boil the potatoes in their skins in boiling salted water for 5 minutes. Drain and when they are cool, peel them and halve lengthways.

COOK'S TIP
Liven up a simple dish of roast or grilled lamb or chicken with these delicious and easy potatoes.

2 Peel the shallots, allowing them to fall into their natural segments. Cut each sweet pepper lengthways into eight strips, discarding seeds and pith.

3 Oil a shallow ovenproof dish thoroughly with olive oil. Arrange the potatoes and peppers in alternating rows and stud with the shallots.

4 Cut the rosemary sprigs into 5cm/2in lengths and tuck among the vegetables. Season the vegetables generously with salt and pepper, add the olive oil and roast, uncovered, for 30–40 minutes until all the vegetables are tender. Turn the vegetables occasionally to cook and brown evenly. Serve hot or at room temperature, with crushed peppercorns.

POTATOES IN A YOGURT SAUCE

TINY POTATOES WITH SKINS ON ARE DELICIOUS IN THIS FAIRLY SPICY YET TANGY YOGURT SAUCE.
SERVE WITH ANY MEAT OR FISH DISH OR JUST WITH HOT CHAPATIS.

SERVES FOUR

INGREDIENTS
12 small new or salad
  potatoes, halved
275g/10oz/1¼ cups natural
  low-fat yogurt
300ml/½ pint/1¼ cups water
1.5ml/¼ tsp turmeric
5ml/1 tsp chilli powder
5ml/1 tsp ground coriander
2.5ml/½ tsp ground cumin
5ml/1 tsp salt
5ml/1 tsp soft brown sugar
30ml/2 tbsp vegetable oil
5ml/1 tsp white cumin seeds
15ml/1 tbsp chopped fresh coriander
2 fresh green chillies, sliced
1 coriander sprig, to garnish
  (optional)

1 Cook the potatoes in their skins in boiling salted water until just tender, then drain and set aside.

2 Mix together the yogurt, water, turmeric, chilli powder, ground coriander, ground cumin, salt and sugar in a bowl. Set aside.

3 Heat the oil in a medium saucepan over a medium-high heat and stir in the white cumin seeds.

4 Reduce the heat to medium, and stir in the prepared yogurt mixture. Cook the sauce, stirring continuously, for about 3 minutes.

5 Add the fresh coriander, green chillies and potatoes to the sauce. Mix well and cook for 5–7 minutes, stirring occasionally.

6 Transfer to a serving dish, garnish with the coriander sprig, if wished and serve hot.

COOK'S TIP
If new or salad potatoes are unavailable, use 450g/1lb ordinary potatoes instead, but not the floury type. Peel them and cut into large chunks, then cook as described above.

POTATO SKEWERS WITH MUSTARD DIP

POTATOES COOKED ON THE BARBECUE HAVE A GREAT FLAVOUR AND CRISP SKIN. TRY THESE DELICIOUS KEBABS SERVED WITH A THICK, GARLIC-RICH DIP.

SERVES FOUR

INGREDIENTS
For the dip
    4 garlic cloves, crushed
    2 egg yolks
    30ml/2 tbsp lemon juice
    300ml/½ pint/1¼ cups extra virgin
      olive oil
    10ml/2 tsp whole-grain mustard
    salt and ground black pepper
For the skewers
    1kg/2¼lb small new potatoes
    200g/7oz shallots, halved
    30ml/2 tbsp olive oil
    15ml/1 tbsp sea salt

1 Prepare the barbecue for cooking the skewers before you begin. To make the dip, place the garlic, egg yolks and lemon juice in a blender or a food processor fitted with the metal blade and process for a few seconds until the mixture is smooth.

2 Keep the blender motor running and add the oil very gradually, pouring it in a thin stream, until the mixture forms a thick, glossy cream. Add the mustard and stir the ingredients together, then season with salt and pepper. Chill until ready to use.

COOK'S TIP
Early or "new" potatoes, and salad potatoes have a firmness necessary to stay on the skewer. Don't be tempted to use other types of small potato, they will probably split or fall off the skewers during cooking.

3 Par-boil the potatoes in their skins in boiling water for 5 minutes. Drain well and then thread them on to metal skewers alternating with the shallots.

4 Brush the skewers with oil and sprinkle with salt. Cook over a barbeque for 10–12 minutes, turning occasionally, Serve with the dip.

BAKED MUSSELS AND POTATOES

THIS IMAGINATIVE BAKED CASSEROLE USES SOME OF THE BEST ITALIAN FLAVOURS — TOMATOES, GARLIC, BASIL AND, OF COURSE, PLUMP, JUICY MUSSELS.

SERVES TWO TO THREE

INGREDIENTS

750g/1¾lb large mussels, in
  their shells
225g/8oz small firm potatoes
75ml/5 tbsp olive oil
2 garlic cloves, finely chopped
8 fresh basil leaves, torn into pieces
2 medium tomatoes, peeled and
  thinly sliced
45ml/3 tbsp breadcrumbs
ground black pepper
basil leaves, to garnish

1 Cut off the "beards" from the mussels. Scrub and soak in several changes of cold water. Discard any with broken shells or ones that are open.

2 Place the mussels with a cupful of water in a large saucepan over a medium heat. As soon as they open, lift them out. Remove and discard the empty half shells, leaving the mussels in the other half. (Discard any mussels that do not open at this stage.) Strain any cooking liquid remaining through a layer of kitchen paper, and reserve to add at the final stage.

3 Cook the potatoes in a large saucepan of boiling water until they are almost tender. Drain and leave to cool. When they are cool enough to handle, peel and slice them.

4 Preheat the oven to 180°C/350°F/ Gas 4. Spread 30ml/2 tbsp of the olive oil in the bottom of a shallow ovenproof dish. Cover with the potato slices in one layer. Add the mussels in their half shells in one layer. Sprinkle with the garlic and basil. Cover with the tomato slices in one layer.

5 Sprinkle with breadcrumbs and black pepper, the reserved mussel cooking liquid and the remaining olive oil. Bake for about 20 minutes until the tomatoes are soft and the breadcrumbs are golden. Serve hot directly from the baking dish, and garnish with basil.

STEAK WITH STOUT AND POTATOES

THE IRISH WAY TO BRAISE BEEF IS IN STOUT OF COURSE AND TOPPED WITH THICKLY SLICED POTATOES. BAKE IT IN A MODERATE OVEN FOR LONG, SLOW TENDERISING IF YOU PREFER.

SERVES FOUR

INGREDIENTS
675g/1½lb stewing beef
15ml/1 tbsp vegetable oil
25g/1oz/2 tbsp butter
225g/8oz tiny white onions
175ml/6fl oz/¾ cup stout or dark beer
300ml/½ pint/1¼ cups beef stock
bouquet garni
675g/1½lb firm, waxy potatoes, cut
  into thick slices
225g/8oz/3 cups large mushrooms,
  sliced
15ml/1 tbsp plain flour
2.5ml/½ tsp mild mustard
salt and ground black pepper
chopped thyme sprigs, to garnish

3 Add the tiny white onions to the pan and cook for 3–4 minutes until lightly browned all over. Return the steak to the pan with the onions. Pour on the stout or beer and stock and season the whole mixture to taste.

5 Add the sliced mushrooms over the potatoes. Cover again and simmer for a further 30 minutes or so. Remove the steak and vegetables with a slotted spoon and arrange on a platter.

1 Trim any excess fat from the steak and cut into four pieces. Season both sides of the meat. Heat the oil and 10g/¼oz/1½ tsp of the butter in a large heavy-based pan.

2 Add the steak and brown on both sides, taking care not to burn the butter. Remove from the pan and set aside.

4 Next add the bouquet garni to the pan and top with the potato slices distributing them evenly over the surface to cover the steak. Bring the ingredients to a boil then reduce the heat, cover with a tight-fitting lid and simmer gently for 1 hour.

VARIATION
For a dish that is lighter, but just as tasty, substitute four lamb leg steaks for the beef, and use dry cider instead of the stout or beer, and lamb or chicken stock instead of beef.

COOK'S TIP
To make onion peeling easier, first put the onions in a bowl and cover with boiling water. Allow them to soak for about 5 minutes and drain. The skins should now peel away easily.

6 Mix the remaining butter with the flour to make a roux. Whisk a little at a time into the cooking liquid in the pan. Stir in the mustard. Cook over a medium heat for 2–3 minutes, stirring all the while, until thickened.

7 Season the sauce and pour over the steak. Garnish with plenty of thyme sprigs and serve the dish at once.

SMOKED HADDOCK AND NEW POTATO PIE

SMOKED HADDOCK HAS A SALTY FLAVOUR AND CAN BE BOUGHT EITHER DYED OR UNDYED. THE DYED FISH HAS A STRONG YELLOW COLOUR WHILE THE OTHER IS ALMOST CREAMY IN COLOUR.

SERVES FOUR

INGREDIENTS
   450g/1lb smoked haddock fillet
   475ml/16fl oz/2 cups
    semi-skimmed milk
   2 bay leaves
   1 onion, quartered
   4 cloves
   450g/1lb new potatoes
   butter, for greasing
   30ml/2 tbsp cornflour
   60ml/4 tbsp double cream
   30ml/2 tbsp chopped fresh chervil
   salt and ground black pepper
   mixed vegetables, to serve

VARIATIONS
Instead of using all smoked haddock for this pie, use half smoked and half fresh. Cook the two types together, as described in Step 1. A generous handful of peeled prawns is a good addition to this pie is you want to make it even more filling.

COOK'S TIP
The fish gives out liquid as it cooks, so it is best to start with a slightly thicker sauce than you might think is necessary.

1 Preheat the oven to 200°C/400°F/ Gas 6. Place the haddock in a deep-sided frying pan. Pour the milk over and add the bay leaves.

2 Stud the onion with the cloves and place it in the pan with the fish and milk. Cover the top and leave to simmer for about 10 minutes or until the fish starts to flake.

3 Remove the fish with a slotted spoon and set aside to cool. Strain the liquid from the pan into a separate saucepan and set aside.

4 To prepare the potatoes, cut them into fine slices, leaving the skins on.

5 Blanch the potatoes in a large saucepan of lightly salted water for 5 minutes. Drain.

6 Grease the base and sides of a 1.2 litre/2 pint/5 cup ovenproof dish. Then using a knife and fork, carefully flake the fish.

7 Reheat the milk in the saucepan. Mix the cornflour with a little water to form a paste and stir in the cream and the chervil. Add to the milk in the pan and cook until thickened.

8 Arrange one-third of the potatoes over the base of the dish and season with pepper. Lay half of the fish over. Repeat layering, finishing with a layer of potatoes on top.

9 Pour the sauce over the top, making sure that it sinks down through the mixture. Cover with foil and cook for 30 minutes. Remove the foil and cook for a further 10 minutes to brown the surface. Serve with a selection of mixed vegetables.

POTATOES WITH BLUE CHEESE AND WALNUTS

FIRM SMALL POTATOES, SERVED IN A CREAMY BLUE CHEESE SAUCE WITH THE CRUNCH OF WALNUTS,
MAKE A GREAT SIDE DISH TO A SIMPLE ROAST MEAL. FOR A CHANGE, SERVE IT AS A LUNCH DISH OR A
LIGHT SUPPER WITH A GREEN SALAD.

SERVES FOUR

INGREDIENTS
    450g/1lb small new or
      salad potatoes
    1 small head of celery, sliced
    1 small red onion, sliced
    115g/4oz/1 cup blue cheese, mashed
    150ml/¼ pint/⅔ cup single cream
    50g/2oz/½ cup walnut pieces
    30ml/2 tbsp chopped fresh parsley
    salt and ground black pepper

COOK'S TIP
Use a combination of blue cheeses, such
as Dolcelatte and Roquefort, or go for the
distinctive flavour of Stilton on its own.
If walnuts are not available, blue cheeses
marry equally well with hazelnuts.

1 Cook the potatoes in their skins in a
large saucepan with plenty of boiling
water for about 15 minutes or until
tender, adding the sliced celery and
onion to the pan for the last 5 minutes
or so of cooking.

2 Drain the vegetables well through a
colander and put them into a shallow
serving dish.

3 In a small saucepan, slowly melt the
cheese in the cream, stirring
occasionally. Do not allow the mixture to
boil but heat it until it scalds.

4 Check the sauce and season to taste.
Pour it evenly over the vegetables in the
dish and scatter over the walnut pieces
and fresh parsley. Serve hot, straight
from the dish.

RACLETTE WITH NEW POTATOES

TRADITIONAL TO BOTH SWITZERLAND AND FRANCE, RACLETTE MELTS TO A VELVETY CREAMINESS AND
WARM GOLDEN COLOUR AND HAS A SAVOURY TASTE WITH A HINT OF SWEETNESS.

SERVES FOUR

INGREDIENTS
For the pickle
    2 red onions, sliced
    5ml/1 tsp sugar
    90ml/6 tbsp red wine vinegar
    2.5ml/½ tsp salt
    generous pinch of dried dill
For the potatoes
    500g/1¼lb new or salad potatoes,
      halved if large
    250g/9oz raclette cheese slices
    salt and ground black pepper

1 To make the pickle spread out the
onions in a glass dish, pour over boiling
water to cover and leave until cold.

2 Meanwhile mix the sugar, vinegar,
salt and dill in a small pan. Heat gently,
stirring, until the sugar has dissolved,
then set aside to cool.

3 Drain the onions and return them to
the dish, pour the vinegar mixture over,
cover and leave for at least 1 hour,
preferably overnight.

4 Cook the potatoes in their skins in
boiling water until tender, then drain
and place in a roasting tin. Preheat the
grill. Season the potatoes and arrange
the raclette on top. Place the tin under
the grill until the cheese melts. Serve
hot. Drain the excess vinegar from the
red onion pickle and serve the pickle
with the potatoes.

COOK'S TIP
To speed up the process look for ready-
sliced raclette for this dish. It is
available from most large supermarkets
and specialist cheese shops.

POTATO AND RED PEPPER FRITTATA

FRITTATA IS LIKE A LARGE OMELETTE, THIS TASTY VERSION IS FILLED WITH POTATOES AND PLENTY OF HERBS. DO USE FRESH MINT IN PREFERENCE TO DRIED IF YOU CAN FIND IT.

SERVES THREE TO FOUR

INGREDIENTS

    450g/1lb small new or
      salad potatoes
    6 eggs
    30ml/2 tbsp chopped fresh mint
    30ml/2 tbsp olive oil
    1 onion, chopped
    2 garlic cloves, crushed
    2 red peppers, seeded and
      roughly chopped
    salt and ground black pepper
    mint sprigs, to garnish

1 Cook the potatoes in their skins in boiling salted water until just tender. Drain and leave to cool slightly, then cut into thick slices.

2 Whisk together the eggs, mint and seasoning in a bowl, then set aside. Heat the oil in a large frying pan.

3 Add the onion, garlic, peppers and potatoes to the pan and cook, stirring occasionally, for 5 minutes.

4 Pour the egg mixture over the vegetables in the frying pan and stir gently.

5 Push the mixture towards the centre of the pan as it cooks to allow the liquid egg to run on to the base. Meanwhile preheat the grill.

6 When the frittata is lightly set, place the pan under the hot grill for 2–3 minutes until the top is a light golden brown colour.

7 Serve hot or cold, cut into wedges piled high on a serving dish and garnished with sprigs of mint.

TURKISH-STYLE NEW POTATO CASSEROLE

*HERE'S A MEAL IN A POT THAT'S SUITABLE FOR FEEDING LARGE NUMBERS OF PEOPLE. IT'S LIGHTLY
SPICED AND HAS PLENTY OF GARLIC — WHO COULD REFUSE?*

SERVES FOUR

INGREDIENTS

60ml/4 tbsp olive oil
1 large onion, chopped
2 small–medium aubergines, cut into
  small cubes
4 courgettes, cut into small chunks
1 green pepper, seeded and chopped
1 red or yellow pepper, seeded
  and chopped
115g/4oz/1 cup fresh or frozen peas
115g/4oz French beans
450g/1lb new or salad
  potatoes, cubed
2.5ml/½ tsp cinnamon
2.5ml/½ tsp ground cumin
5ml/1 tsp paprika
4–5 tomatoes, skinned
400g/14oz can chopped tomatoes
30ml/2 tbsp chopped fresh parsley
3–4 garlic cloves, crushed
350ml/12fl oz/1½ cups
  vegetable stock
salt and ground black pepper
black olives, to garnish
fresh parsley, to garnish

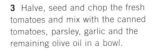

1 Preheat the oven to 190°C/375°F/
Gas 5. Heat 45ml/3 tbsp of the oil in a
heavy-based pan, add the onion and fry
until golden. Add the aubergines, sauté
for about 3 minutes and then add the
courgettes, green and red or yellow
peppers, peas, beans and potatoes,
together with the spices and seasoning.

2 Continue to cook for 3 minutes,
stirring all the time. Transfer to a
shallow ovenproof dish.

3 Halve, seed and chop the fresh
tomatoes and mix with the canned
tomatoes, parsley, garlic and the
remaining olive oil in a bowl.

4 Pour the stock over the aubergine
mixture and then spoon over the
prepared tomato mixture.

5 Cover and bake the dish for 30–45
minutes until the vegetables are tender.
Serve hot, garnished with black olives
and parsley.

MAINCROP
POTATOES

While the year continues apace, the potatoes underground swell and firm up.
The skin becomes thick enough to withstand storage through the long maincrop
season and often well into the following year. The flesh of many
maincrop potatoes becomes soft and floury; a characteristic crucial for the
perfect mash; for easily making delicious soups, such as Cream of Cauliflower,
or North African Spiced soup; for creating fluffy, light fish pie toppings;
or for adding to dough to make delicious bread.
Maincrop potatoes can be fairly firm too and are suited to making the grated
classic Latkes, a Jewish potato pancake which needs to be fried until golden and
crisp without falling to pieces before it's cooked through. Above all, maincrop
potatoes are versatile; ideal for many dishes throughout their long season.

CHILLED LEEK AND POTATO SOUP

THIS CREAMY-SMOOTH COLD VERSION OF THE CLASSIC VICHYSSOISE IS SERVED WITH THE REFRESHING TANG OF YOGURT AS A TOPPING.

SERVES FOUR

INGREDIENTS

25g/1oz/2 tbsp butter
15ml/1 tbsp vegetable oil
1 small onion, chopped
3 leeks, sliced
2 medium floury potatoes, diced
600ml/1 pint/2½ cups
  vegetable stock
300ml/½ pint/1¼ cups milk
45ml/3 tbsp single cream
a little extra milk (optional)
salt and ground black pepper
60ml/4 tbsp natural yogurt and
  fried chopped leeks, to serve

1 Heat the butter and oil in a large pan and add the onion, leeks and potatoes. Cover and cook for 15 minutes, stirring occasionally. Bring to the boil, reduce the heat and simmer for 10 minutes.

2 Stir in the stock and milk and cover again.

3 Ladle the vegetables and liquid into a blender or a food processor in batches and purée until smooth. Return to the pan, stir in the cream and season.

4 Leave the soup to cool, and then chill for 3–4 hours. You may need to add a little extra milk to thin down the soup, as it will thicken slightly as it cools.

5 Ladle the soup into soup bowls and serve topped with a spoonful of natural yogurt and a sprinkling of leeks.

SWEETCORN AND POTATO CHOWDER

THIS CREAMY YET CHUNKY SOUP IS RICH WITH THE SWEET TASTE OF CORN. IT'S EXCELLENT SERVED WITH THICK CRUSTY BREAD AND TOPPED WITH SOME MELTED CHEDDAR CHEESE.

SERVES FOUR

INGREDIENTS
   1 onion, chopped
   1 garlic clove, crushed
   1 medium baking potato, chopped
   2 celery sticks, sliced
   1 small green pepper, seeded, halved
      and sliced
   30ml/2 tbsp sunflower oil
   25g/1oz/2 tbsp butter
   600ml/1 pint/2½ cups stock or water
   300ml/½ pint/1¼ cups milk
   200g/7oz can flageolet beans
   300g/11oz can sweetcorn kernels
   good pinch dried sage
   salt and ground black pepper
   Cheddar cheese, grated, to serve

1 Put the onion, garlic, potato, celery and green pepper into a large heavy-based saucepan with the oil and butter.

2 Heat the ingredients in a large saucepan until sizzling then reduce the heat to low. Cover and cook gently for about 10 minutes, shaking the pan occasionally.

3 Pour in the stock or water, season with salt and pepper to taste and bring to the boil. Reduce the heat, cover again and simmer gently for about 15 minutes until the vegetables are tender.

4 Add the milk, beans and sweetcorn – including their liquids – and the sage. Simmer, uncovered, for 5 minutes. Check the seasoning and serve hot, sprinkled with grated cheese.

CREAM OF CAULIFLOWER SOUP

THIS SOUP IS LIGHT IN FLAVOUR YET SATISFYING ENOUGH FOR A LUNCHTIME SNACK.
YOU CAN TRY GREEN CAULIFLOWER FOR A COLOURFUL CHANGE.

SERVES SIX

INGREDIENTS
    30ml/2 tbsp olive oil
    2 large onions, finely diced
    1 garlic clove, crushed
    3 large floury potatoes, finely diced
    3 celery sticks, finely diced
    1.75 litres/3 pints/7½ cups
      vegetable stock
    2 carrots, finely diced
    1 medium cauliflower, chopped
    15ml/1 tbsp chopped fresh dill
    15ml/1 tbsp lemon juice
    5ml/1 tsp mustard powder
    1.5ml/¼ tsp caraway seeds
    300ml/½ pint/1¼ cups single cream
    salt and ground black pepper
    shredded spring onions, to garnish

3 Add the cauliflower, fresh dill, lemon juice, mustard powder and caraway seeds and simmer for 20 minutes.

4 Process the soup in a blender or food processor until smooth, return to the saucepan and stir in the cream. Season to taste and serve garnished with shredded spring onions.

1 Heat the oil in a large saucepan, add the onions and garlic and fry them for a few minutes until they soften. Add the potatoes, celery and stock and simmer for 10 minutes.

2 Add the carrots and simmer for a further 10 minutes.

NORTH AFRICAN SPICED SOUP

CLASSICALLY KNOWN AS HARIRA, THIS SOUP IS OFTEN SERVED IN THE EVENING DURING RAMADAN, THE MUSLIM RELIGIOUS FESTIVAL WHEN FOLLOWERS FAST DURING THE DAYTIME FOR A MONTH.

SERVES SIX

INGREDIENTS

1 large onion, chopped
1.2 litres/2 pints/5 cups
  vegetable stock
5ml/1 tsp ground cinnamon
5ml/1 tsp turmeric
15ml/1 tbsp grated ginger
pinch cayenne pepper
2 carrots, diced
2 celery sticks, diced
400g/14oz can chopped tomatoes
450g/1lb floury potatoes, diced
5 strands saffron
400g/14oz can chick-peas, drained
30ml/2 tbsp chopped fresh coriander
15ml/1 tbsp lemon juice
salt and ground black pepper
fried wedges of lemon, to serve

1 Place the onion in a large pot with 300ml/½ pint/1¼ cups of the vegetable stock. Simmer gently for about 10 minutes.

2 Meanwhile, mix together the cinnamon, turmeric, ginger, cayenne pepper and 30ml/2 tbsp of stock to form a paste. Stir into the onion mixture with the carrots, celery and remaining stock.

3 Bring the mixture to a boil, reduce the heat, then cover and gently simmer for 5 minutes.

4 Add the tomatoes and potatoes and simmer gently, covered, for 20 minutes. Add the saffron, chick-peas, coriander and lemon juice. Season to taste and when piping hot serve with fried wedges of lemon.

BERRICHONNE POTATOES

A POTATO DISH WITH A DIFFERENCE. THE TOP OF THE POTATOES WILL BE CRISPY WITH A SOFTLY COOKED BASE IN THE STOCK, ONIONS AND BACON.

SERVES FOUR

INGREDIENTS
   900g/2 lb maincrop potatoes
   25g/1oz/2 tbsp butter
   1 onion, finely chopped
   115g/4oz unsmoked streaky bacon,
      rinds removed
   350ml/12fl oz /1½ cups
      vegetable stock
   chopped parsley, to garnish
   sea salt and ground black pepper

1   Preheat the oven to 200°C/400°F/ Gas 6. Peel the potatoes and trim them into barrel shapes. Leave the potatoes to stand in a bowl of cold water.

2   Melt the butter in a frying pan. Add the onions, stir and cover with a lid. Cook for 2–3 minutes, until they are soft but not brown.

3   Chop the bacon and add to the onions, cover and cook for 2 minutes.

4   Spoon the onion mixture into the base of a 1.5 litres /2½ pints/6¼ cups rectangular shallow ovenproof dish. Lay the potatoes over the onion mixture and pour the stock over, making sure that it comes halfway up the sides of them. Season and cook for 1 hour. Garnish with chopped parsley.

POLPETTES

Yummy little fried mouthfuls of potato and tangy-sharp Greek feta cheese, flavoured with dill and lemon juice. Serve as a starter or party bite.

SERVES FOUR

INGREDIENTS

  500g/1¼lb floury potatoes
  115g/4oz/1 cup feta cheese
  4 spring onions, chopped
  45ml/3 tbsp chopped fresh dill
  1 egg, beaten
  15ml/1 tbsp lemon juice
  salt and ground black pepper
  plain flour, for dredging
  45ml/3 tbsp olive oil
  dill sprigs, to garnish
  shredded spring onions, to garnish
  lemon wedges, to serve

1 Cook the potatoes in their skins in boiling lightly salted water until soft. Drain and leave to cool slightly, then chop them in half and peel while still warm.

2 Place in a bowl and mash. Crumble the feta cheese into the potatoes and add the spring onions, dill, egg and lemon juice and season with salt and pepper. (The cheese is salty, so taste before you add salt.) Stir well.

3 Cover and chill until firm. Divide the mixture into walnut-size balls, then flatten them slightly. Dredge with flour, shaking off the excess.

4 Heat the oil in a frying pan and fry the polpettes in batches until golden brown on both sides. Drain on kitchen paper and serve hot, garnished with spring onions, dill and lemon wedges.

POTATO LATKES

LATKES ARE TRADITIONAL JEWISH POTATO PANCAKES, FRIED UNTIL GOLDEN AND CRISP AND SERVED WITH HOT SALT BEEF OR APPLE SAUCE AND SOURED CREAM.

SERVES FOUR

INGREDIENTS
  2 medium floury potatoes
  1 onion
  1 large egg, beaten
  30ml/2 tbsp medium-ground
    matzo meal
  vegetable oil, for frying
  salt and ground black pepper

1 Coarsely grate the potatoes and the onion. Put them in a large colander but don't rinse them. Press them down, squeezing out as much of the thick starchy liquid as possible. Transfer the potato mixture to a bowl.

2 Immediately stir in the beaten egg. Add the matzo meal, stirring gently to mix. Season with salt and plenty of pepper.

VARIATION
Try using equal quantities of potatoes and Jerusalem artichokes for a really distinct flavour.

3 Heat a 1cm/½in layer of oil in a heavy-based frying pan for a few minutes (test it by throwing in a small piece of bread – it should sizzle). Take a spoonful of the potato mixture and lower it carefully into the oil. Continue adding spoonfuls, leaving space between each one.

4 Flatten the pancakes slightly with the back of a spoon. Fry for a few minutes until the latkes are golden brown on the underside, carefully turn them over and continue frying until golden brown.

5 Drain the latkes on kitchen paper, then transfer to an ovenproof serving dish and keep warm in a low oven while frying the remainder. Serve hot.

SWISS SOUFFLÉ POTATOES

A FABULOUS COMBINATION OF RICH AND SATISFYING INGREDIENTS — CHEESE, EGGS, CREAM,
BUTTER AND POTATOES. THIS IS PERFECT FOR COLD-WEATHER EATING.

SERVES FOUR

INGREDIENTS

   4 floury baking potatoes
   115g/4oz/1 cup Gruyère
    cheese, grated
   115g/4oz/8 tbsp herb-flavoured butter
   60ml/4 tbsp double cream
   2 eggs, separated
   salt and ground black pepper

1 Preheat the oven to 220°C/425°F/
Gas 7. Prick the potatoes all over with a
fork. Bake for 1–1½ hours until tender.
Remove them from the oven and reduce
the temperature to 180°C/350°F/Gas 4.

2 Cut each potato in half and scoop
out the flesh into a bowl. Return the
potato shells to the oven to crisp them
up while making the filling.

3 Mash the potato flesh using a fork,
then add the Gruyère, herb-flavoured
butter, cream, egg yolks and seasoning.
Beat well until smooth.

4 Whisk the egg whites in a separate
bowl until they hold stiff but not dry
peaks, then carefully fold into the
potato mixture.

5 Pile the mixture back into the potato
shells and place on a baking sheet.
Bake in the oven for 20–25 minutes
until risen and golden brown.

6 Serve the potatoes hot, sprinkled with
fresh, snipped chives, if wished, and a
bowl of mayonnaise to the side.

BIARRITZ POTATOES

A COMBINATION OF CLASSIC MASHED POTATOES WITH FINELY DICED HAM AND PEPPERS MIXED IN.
THIS DISH IS GREAT SERVED WITH ROASTED CHICKEN.

SERVES FOUR

INGREDIENTS
    900g/2lb floury potatoes
    50g/2oz/4 tbsp butter
    90ml/6 tbsp milk
    50g/2oz cooked ham, finely diced
    1 red pepper, deseeded and
      finely diced
    15ml/1tbsp chopped fresh parsley
    sea salt and ground black pepper

1 Peel and cut the potatoes into chunks. Boil in lightly salted water for 20 minutes or until very tender.

2 Drain and return the potatoes to the pan and allow the steam to dry off over a low heat.

3 Either mash or pass the potatoes through a potato ricer. Add the butter and milk and stir in the cooked ham, peppers and parsley. Season and serve.

LYONNAISE POTATOES

TWO SIMPLE INGREDIENTS ARE PREPARED SEPARATELY AND THEN TOSSED TOGETHER TO CREATE THE
PERFECT COMBINATION. THESE POTATOES GO VERY WELL WITH A SIMPLE MEAT DISH, SUCH AS STEAK
OR PORK CHOPS. SERVE WITH A BOWL OF FRENCH BEANS, TOSSED IN BUTTER.

SERVES SIX

INGREDIENTS
    900g/2lb floury potatoes
    vegetable oil for shallow frying
    25g/1oz/2 tbsp butter
    15ml/1 tbsp olive oil
    2 medium onions, sliced into rings
    sea salt
    15ml/1 tbsp chopped fresh parsley

VARIATION
For a more substantial version of this dish, ham or bacon can be added. Use about 50g/2oz chopped roast ham or bacon and fry with the onions until cooked through.

1 Scrub the potatoes clean and cook in a large saucepan with plenty of boiling water for 10 minutes.

2 Drain the potatoes through a colander and leave to cool slightly. When the potatoes are cool enough to handle, peel and finely slice them.

3 Heat the vegetable oil and shallow fry the potatoes in two batches for about 10 minutes until crisp, turning occasionally.

4 Meanwhile, melt the butter with the oil in a frying pan and fry the onions for 10 minutes until golden. Drain on kitchen paper.

5 Remove the potatoes with a slotted spoon and drain on kitchen paper. Toss with sea salt and carefully mix with the onions. Sprinkle with the parsley.

POTATO, BEEF, BEETROOT AND MUSHROOM GRATIN

THIS VARIATION OF AN UNUSUAL POLISH MIX OF FLAVOURS PRODUCES A VERY HEARTY MAIN MEAL. HORSERADISH AND MUSTARD ARE GREAT WITH BOTH THE BEEF AND THE BEETROOT, MOST OF WHICH IS HIDDEN UNDERNEATH MAKING A COLOURFUL SURPRISE WHEN YOU SERVE IT.

SERVES FOUR

INGREDIENTS
30ml/2 tbsp vegetable oil
1 small onion, chopped
15ml/1 tbsp plain flour
150ml/¼ pint/⅔ cup vegetable stock
225g/8oz cooked beetroot, drained
  well and chopped
15ml/1 tbsp creamed horseradish
15ml/1 tbsp caraway seeds
3 shallots, or 1 medium
  onion, chopped
450g/1lb frying or grilling steak, cut
  into thin strips
225g/8oz assorted wild or cultivated
  mushrooms, sliced
10–15ml/2–3 tsp hot mustard
60ml/4 tbsp soured cream
45ml/3 tbsp chopped fresh parsley
For the potato border
900g/2lb floury potatoes
150ml/¼ pint/⅔ cup milk
25g/1oz/2 tbsp butter or margarine
15ml/1 tbsp chopped fresh dill
  (optional)
salt and ground black pepper

1 Preheat the oven to 190ºC/375ºF/ Gas 5. Lightly oil a baking or gratin dish. Heat 15ml/1 tbsp of the oil in a large saucepan, add the onion and fry until softened but not coloured. Stir in the flour, remove from the heat and gradually add the stock, stirring until well blended and smooth.

2 Return to the heat and simmer until thickened, stirring all the while. Add the beetroot (reserve a few pieces for the topping, if you wish), horseradish and caraway seeds. Mix gently, then put to one side.

3 To make the potato border, first cook the potatoes in a large saucepan with plenty of boiling salted water for 20 minutes until tender. Drain well through a colander and mash with the milk and butter or margarine. Add the chopped dill, if using, and season the mixture with salt and pepper to taste. Stir to combine the seasonings.

COOK'S TIP
If planning ahead, for instance for a dinner party, this entire dish can be made in advance and heated through when needed. Allow 50 minutes baking time from room temperature. Add the beetroot pieces to the topping near the end of the cooking time.

4 Spoon the potatoes into the prepared dish and push well up the sides, making a large hollow in the middle for the filling. Spoon the beetroot mixture into the well, evening it out with the back of a spoon and set aside.

5 Heat the remaining oil in a large frying pan, add the shallots or onion and fry until softened but not coloured. Add the steak and stir-fry quickly until browned all over. Then add the mushrooms and fry quickly until most of their juices have cooked away. Remove the pan from the heat and gently stir in the mustard, soured cream, seasoning to taste and half the parsley until well blended.

6 Spoon the steak mixture over the beetroot mixture in the baking dish, sprinkling the reserved beetroot over the top, cover and bake for 30 minutes. Serve hot, sprinkled with the remaining parsley.

LAMB PIE WITH MUSTARD THATCH

SHEPHERD'S PIE WITH A TWIST, THE MUSTARD GIVING A REAL TANG TO THE POTATO TOPPING.

2 Fry the lamb in a non-stick pan, breaking it up with a fork, until lightly browned all over. Add the onion, celery and carrots to the pan and cook for 2–3 minutes, stirring, to stop the mixture sticking to the base.

3 Stir in the stock and cornflour mixture. Bring to the boil, stirring all the while, then remove from the heat. Stir in the Worcestershire sauce and rosemary and season with salt and pepper to taste.

4 Turn the lamb mixture into a 1.75 litre/3 pint/7 cup ovenproof dish and spread over the potato topping evenly, swirling with the edge of a palette knife. Bake for 30–35 minutes until golden on the top. Serve hot with a selection of fresh vegetables.

SERVES FOUR

INGREDIENTS

800g/1¾lb floury potatoes, diced
60ml/4 tbsp milk
15ml/1 tbsp whole-grain or
    French mustard
a little butter
450g/1lb lean lamb, minced
1 onion, chopped
2 celery sticks, thinly sliced
2 carrots, diced
30ml/2 tbsp cornflour blended into
    150ml/¼ pint/⅔ cup lamb stock
15ml/1 tbsp Worcestershire sauce
30ml/2 tbsp chopped fresh rosemary,
    or 10ml/2 tsp dried
salt and ground black pepper
fresh vegetables, to serve

1 Cook the potatoes in a large saucepan of boiling lightly salted water until tender. Drain well and mash until smooth, then stir in the milk, mustard, butter and seasoning to taste. Meanwhile preheat the oven to 200°C/400°F/Gas 6.

VARIATION
Although the original shepherd's pie is made with lamb, most people make it with minced beef as well. To vary the potato topping slightly, try adding horseradish – either creamed or for an even stronger flavour, freshly grated.

STOVED CHICKEN

"STOVIES" WERE ORIGINALLY — NOT SURPRISINGLY — POTATOES SLOWLY COOKED ON THE STOVE WITH ONIONS AND DRIPPING OR BUTTER UNTIL FALLING TO PIECES. THIS VERSION INCLUDES A DELICIOUS LAYER OF BACON AND CHICKEN HIDDEN IN THE MIDDLE OF THE VEGETABLES.

SERVES FOUR

INGREDIENTS

    butter, for greasing
    1kg/2¼lb baking potatoes, cut into
      5mm/¼in slices
    2 large onions, thinly sliced
    15ml/1 tbsp chopped fresh thyme
    25g/1oz/2 tbsp butter
    15ml/1 tbsp vegetable oil
    2 large bacon slices, chopped
    4 large chicken joints, halved
    600ml/1 pint/2½ cups chicken stock
    1 bay leaf
    salt and ground black pepper

COOK'S TIP
Instead of chicken joints, choose eight chicken thighs or chicken drumsticks.

1 Preheat the oven to 150°C/300°F/ Gas 2. Arrange a thick layer of half the potato slices in the bottom of a large lightly greased heavy-based casserole, then cover with half the onions. Sprinkle with half of the thyme, and season with salt and pepper to taste.

2 Heat the butter and oil in a large heavy-based frying pan, add the bacon and chicken, stirring frequently, and brown on all sides. Using a slotted spoon, transfer the chicken and bacon to the casserole. Reserve the fat in the pan.

3 Sprinkle the remaining thyme over the chicken, season with salt and pepper, then cover with the remaining onion slices, followed by a neat layer of overlapping potato slices. Season the dish well.

4 Pour the stock into the casserole, add the bay leaf and brush the potatoes with the reserved fat. Cover tightly and bake for about 2 hours until the chicken is very tender.

5 Preheat the grill. Take the cover off the casserole and place it under the grill until the slices of potato are beginning to turn golden brown and crisp. Remove the bay leaf and serve hot.

COD, BASIL, TOMATO AND POTATO PIE

*NATURAL AND SMOKED FISH MAKE A GREAT COMBINATION, ESPECIALLY WITH THE HINT OF TOMATO
AND BASIL. SERVED WITH A GREEN SALAD, IT MAKES AN IDEAL DISH FOR LUNCH OR A FAMILY SUPPER.*

2 Melt 75g/3oz/6 tbsp of the butter in a
large pan, add the onion and cook for
about 5 minutes until softened and
tender but not browned. Sprinkle over
the flour and half the chopped basil.
Gradually add the reserved fish cooking
liquid, adding a little more milk if
necessary to make a fairly thin sauce,
stirring constantly to make a smooth
consistency. Bring to the boil, season
with salt and pepper, and add the
remaining basil.

3 Remove the pan from the heat, then
add the fish and tomatoes and stir
gently to combine. Pour into an
ovenproof dish.

SERVES EIGHT

INGREDIENTS
   1kg/2¼lb smoked cod
   1kg/2¼lb white cod
   900ml/1½ pint/3¾ cups milk
   1.2litres/2 pints/5 cups water
   2 basil sprigs
   1 lemon thyme sprig
   150g/5oz/10 tbsp butter
   1 onion, chopped
   75g/3oz/⅔ cup plain flour
   30ml/2 tbsp chopped fresh basil
   4 firm plum tomatoes, peeled
    and chopped
   12 medium maincrop floury potatoes
   salt and ground black pepper
   crushed black pepper corns,
    to garnish
   lettuce leaves, to serve

1 Place both kinds of fish in a roasting
tin with 600ml/1 pint/2½ cups of the
milk, the water and the herb sprigs.
Bring to a simmer and cook gently for
about 3–4 minutes. Leave the fish to
cool in the liquid for about 20 minutes.
Drain the fish, reserving the cooking
liquid for use in the sauce. Flake the
fish, removing any skin and bone.

4 Preheat the oven to 180°C/350°F/
Gas 4. Cook the potatoes in boiling
water until tender. Drain then add the
remaining butter and milk, and mash.
Season to taste and spoon over the fish
mixture, using a fork to create a
pattern. You can freeze the pie at this
stage. Bake for 30 minutes until the top
is golden. Sprinkle with the crushed
pepper corns and serve hot with lettuce.

CLASSIC FISH PIE

ORIGINALLY A FISH PIE WAS BASED ON THE "CATCH OF THE DAY". NOW WE CAN CHOOSE EITHER THE FISH WE LIKE BEST, OR THE VARIETY THAT OFFERS BEST VALUE FOR MONEY.

SERVES FOUR

INGREDIENTS
   butter, for greasing
   450g/1lb mixed fish, such as
      cod or salmon fillets and
      peeled prawns
   finely grated rind of 1 lemon
   450g/1lb floury potatoes
   25g/1oz/2 tbsp butter
   salt and ground black pepper
   1 egg, beaten
For the sauce
   15g/½oz/1 tbsp butter
   15ml/1 tbsp plain flour
   150ml/¼ pint/⅔ cup milk
   45ml/3 tbsp chopped fresh parsley

1 Preheat the oven to 220°C/425°F/
Gas 7. Grease an ovenproof dish and
set aside. Cut the fish into bite-sized
pieces. Season the fish, sprinkle over
the lemon rind and place in the base of
the prepared dish. Allow to sit while you
make the topping.

2 Cook the potatoes in boiling salted
water until tender.

3 Meanwhile make the sauce. Melt the
butter in a saucepan, add the flour and
cook, stirring, for a few minutes.
Remove from the heat and gradually
whisk in the milk. Return to the heat
and bring to the boil then reduce the
heat and simmer, whisking all the time,
until the sauce has thickened and
achieved a smooth consistency. Add the
parsley and season to taste. Pour over
the fish mixture.

4 Drain the potatoes well and then
mash with the butter.

5 Pipe or spoon the potatoes on top of
the fish mixture. Brush the beaten egg
over the potatoes. Bake for 45 minutes
until the top is golden brown. Serve hot.

COOK'S TIP
If using frozen fish defrost it very well
first, as lots of water will ruin your pie.

BUBBLE AND SQUEAK

WHETHER YOU HAVE LEFTOVERS, OR COOK THIS OLD-FASHIONED CLASSIC FROM FRESH, BE SURE TO GIVE IT A REALLY GOOD "SQUEAK" (FRY) IN THE PAN SO IT TURNS A RICH HONEY BROWN AS ALL THE FLAVOURS CARAMELIZE TOGETHER. IT IS KNOWN AS COLCANNON IN IRELAND, WHERE IT IS TURNED IN CHUNKS OR SECTIONS, PRODUCING A CREAMY BROWN AND WHITE CAKE.

SERVES FOUR

INGREDIENTS
    60ml/4 tbsp dripping, bacon fat or
      vegetable oil
    1 onion, finely chopped
    450g/1lb floury potatoes, cooked
      and mashed
    225g/8oz cooked cabbage or Brussels
      sprouts, finely chopped
    salt and ground black pepper

1 Heat 30ml/2 tbsp of the dripping, fat or oil in a heavy-based frying pan. Add the onion and cook, stirring frequently, until softened but not browned.

2 In a large bowl, mix together the potatoes and cooked cabbage or sprouts and season with salt and plenty of pepper to taste.

3 Add the vegetables to the pan with the cooked onions, stir well, then press the vegetable mixture into a large, even cake.

4 Cook over a medium heat for about 15 minutes until the cake is browned underneath.

5 Invert a large plate over the pan, and, holding it tightly against the pan, turn them both over together. Lift off the frying pan, return it to the heat and add the remaining dripping, fat or oil. When hot, slide the cake back into the pan, browned side uppermost.

6 Cook over a medium heat for 10 minutes or until the underside is golden brown. Serve hot, in wedges.

COOK'S TIP
If you don't have leftover cooked cabbage or Brussels sprouts, shred raw cabbage and cook both in boiling salted water until tender. Drain, then chop.

BAKED SCALLOPED POTATOES WITH FETA CHEESE AND OLIVES

THINLY SLICED POTATOES ARE COOKED WITH GREEK FETA CHEESE AND BLACK AND GREEN OLIVES IN OLIVE OIL. THIS DISH IS A GOOD ONE TO SERVE WITH TOASTED PITTA BREAD.

SERVES FOUR

INGREDIENTS

900g/2lb maincrop potatoes
150ml/¼ pint/⅔ cup olive oil
1 sprig rosemary
275g/10oz/2½ cups feta cheese, crumbled
115g/4oz/1 cup pitted black and green olives
300ml/½ pint/1¼ cups hot vegetable stock
salt and ground black pepper

COOK'S TIP
Make sure you choose Greek feta cheese, which has a completely different texture to Danish.

1 Preheat the oven to 200°C/400°F/ Gas 6. Cook the potatoes in plenty of boiling water for 15 minutes. Drain and cool slightly. Peel the potatoes and cut into thin slices.

2 Brush the base and sides of a 1.5 litre/2½ pint/6¼ cup rectangular ovenproof dish with some of the olive oil.

3 Layer the potatoes in the dish with the rosemary, cheese and olives. Drizzle with the remaining olive oil and pour over the stock. Season the whole with salt and plenty of ground black pepper.

4 Cook for 35 minutes, covering with foil to prevent the potatoes from getting too brown. Serve hot, straight from the dish.

BAKED POTATOES AND THREE FILLINGS

POTATOES BAKED IN THEIR SKINS UNTIL THEY ARE CRISP ON THE OUTSIDE AND FLUFFY IN THE MIDDLE MAKE AN EXCELLENT AND NOURISHING MEAL ON THEIR OWN. BUT FOR AN EVEN BETTER TREAT, ADD ONE OF THESE DELICIOUS AND EASY TOPPINGS.

SERVES FOUR

INGREDIENTS
    4 medium baking potatoes
    olive oil
    sea salt
    filling of your choice (see below)

COOK'S TIP
Choose potatoes which are evenly sized and have undamaged skins, and scrub them thoroughly. If they are done before you are ready to serve them, take them out of the oven and wrap them up in a warmed cloth until they are needed.

1 Preheat the oven to 200°C/400°F/ Gas 6. Score the potatoes with a cross and rub all over with the olive oil.

2 Place on a baking sheet and cook for 45 minutes to 1 hour until a knife inserted into the centres indicates they are cooked. Or cook in the microwave according to your manufacturer's instructions.

3 Cut the potatoes open along the score lines and push up the flesh. Season and fill with your chosen filling.

STIR-FRY VEG
    45ml/3 tbsp groundnut or sunflower oil
    2 leeks, thinly sliced
    2 carrots, cut into sticks
    1 courgette, thinly sliced
    115g/4oz baby corn, halved
    115g/4oz/1½ cup button mushrooms, sliced
    45ml/3 tbsp soy sauce
    30ml/2 tbsp dry sherry or vermouth
    15ml/1 tbsp sesame oil
    sesame seeds, to garnish

1 Heat the groundnut or sunflower oil in a wok or large frying pan until really hot. Add the leeks, carrots, courgette and baby corn and stir-fry together for about 2 minutes, then add the mushrooms and stir-fry for a further minute. Mix the soy sauce, sherry or vermouth and sesame oil and pour over the vegetables. Heat through until just bubbling and scatter the sesame seeds over.

RED BEAN CHILLIES
    425g/15oz can red kidney beans, drained
    200g/7oz/scant 1 cup low-fat cottage or cream cheese
    30ml/2 tbsp mild chilli sauce
    5ml/1 tsp ground cumin

1 Heat the beans in a pan or microwave and stir in the cottage or cream cheese, chilli sauce and cumin.

2 Serve topped with more chilli sauce.

CHEESE AND CREAMY CORN
    425g/15oz can creamed corn
    115g/4oz/1 cup hard cheese, grated
    5ml/1 tsp mixed dried herbs
    fresh parsley sprigs, to garnish

1 Heat the corn gently with the cheese and mixed herbs until well blended.

2 Use to fill the potatoes and garnish with fresh parsley sprigs.

POTATO BREAD WITH CARAMELISED ONIONS AND ROSEMARY

THE ROSEMARY AND ONIONS INCORPORATED INTO THIS BREAD GIVE IT A MEDITERRANEAN FEEL.
IT IS DELICIOUS SERVED WARM WITH A SIMPLE VEGETABLE SOUP.

MAKES A 900G/2LB LOAF

INGREDIENTS
    450g/1lb/4 cups strong white flour
    5ml/1 tsp easy-blend dried yeast
    a pinch of salt, for the dough
    15g/½oz/1 tbsp butter
    325ml/11fl oz/1⅓ cups warmed milk
    15ml/1 tbsp olive oil
    2 medium onions, sliced into rings
    115g/4oz maincrop potatoes, grated
    1 sprig rosemary, chopped
    2.5ml/½ tsp sea salt
    oil, for greasing and to serve

1 Sift the flour into a large bowl. Make a well in the centre and stir in the yeast and a pinch of salt. Rub in the butter until the mixture resembles fine breadcrumbs and then gradually pour in the lukewarm milk.

2 Stir the mixture with a round-bladed knife and then once the wet ingredients have become incorporated, bring it together with your fingers.

3 Turn the dough out and knead on a surface dusted with flour for 5 minutes or until the dough is smooth and elastic. Return the bread to a clean bowl and cover with a damp cloth. Leave to rise in a warm place for 45 minutes or until the dough has doubled in size.

4 Meanwhile, heat the oil in a saucepan and add the onions, stir over a low heat and cook for about 20 minutes until the onions are golden brown and very soft. Set aside.

5 Bring a saucepan of lightly salted water to the boil and add the grated potatoes to the pan. Cook for 5 minutes or until just tender. Drain and plunge into cold water.

VARIATION
For a more piquant flavour, add some bottled sundried tomatoes, drained of their oil and chopped, and a scattering of pitted black olives to the onion layers. Try fresh thyme for a subtle herby tang.

6 Turn the dough out of the bowl and knock back. Roll out on a lightly floured surface. Drain the potatoes and scatter half over the surface with a little rosemary and half the onions. Carefully roll the dough up into a sausage shape.

7 Lift the dough into an oiled 23 x 23cm/9 x 9in tin. Using the palms of your hands flatten the dough out, making sure that the dough fits the tin neatly. Scatter the remaining potatoes and onions over the top with the sea salt and rosemary.

8 Cover again with a damp cloth and leave to rise for 20 minutes.

9 Meanwhile, preheat the oven to 220°C/425°F/Gas 7. Bake the bread for 15–20 minutes. Serve warm drizzled with a little extra olive oil.

COOK'S TIP
If you don't like your onions very crisp, cover the loaf with foil after 10 minutes to prevent the surface from over-browning. Use the largest grater setting available on the food processor for the potatoes, to keep them from becoming too sticky when blanched.

SWEET POTATOES

Although no relation to the potato, the sweet potato cooks up in exactly the same way and has all the same characteristics, although the time it takes to cook is often lengthier. The two main varieties of sweet potatoes are both a recognizable yellowish orange colour.

The flesh of sweet potatoes has a soft texture which can be cooked up in numerous ways. In hotter countries where sweet potatoes originated they are frequently served with lightly spiced foods. They are often found in fish dishes, such as Sweet Potato Fish Rolls and also partner strong savoury flavours such as bacon well. The traditional American dish, Orange Candied Sweet Potatoes, is flavoured with maple syrup and spices, and served with turkey at Thanksgiving.

The very name of the vegetable hints at a sweetness that inclines cooks to use sweet potatoes in baking too. Sweet potatoes are delicious in bread rolls or scones, and taste superb as Sweet Potato Muffins.

BAKED SWEET POTATO SALAD

THIS SALAD HAS A TRULY TROPICAL TASTE AND IS IDEAL SERVED WITH ASIAN OR CARIBBEAN DISHES.

SERVES FOUR TO SIX

INGREDIENTS

1kg/2¼lb sweet potatoes

For the dressing

45ml/3 tbsp chopped fresh coriander

juice of 1 lime

150ml/¼ pint/⅔ cup natural yogurt

For the salad

1 red pepper, seeded and
finely diced

3 celery sticks, finely diced

¼ red skinned onion, finely chopped

1 red chilli, finely chopped

salt and ground black pepper

coriander leaves, to garnish

1 Preheat the oven to 200°C/400°F/ Gas 6. Wash and pierce the potatoes all over and bake in the oven for 40 minutes or until tender.

2 Meanwhile, mix the dressing ingredients together in a bowl and season to taste. Chill while you prepare the remaining ingredients.

3 In a large bowl mix the red pepper, celery, onion and chilli together.

4 Remove the potatoes from the oven and when cool enough to handle, peel them. Cut the potatoes into cubes and add them to the bowl. Drizzle the dressing over and toss carefully. Season again to taste and serve, garnished with fresh coriander.

GLAZED SWEET POTATOES WITH BACON

SMOKY BACON IS THE PERFECT ADDITION TO THESE MELT-IN-THE-MOUTH SUGAR-TOPPED POTATOES.
THEY TASTE GREAT AS A CHANGE FROM ROAST POTATOES, WITH ROAST DUCK OR CHICKEN.

SERVES FOUR TO SIX

INGREDIENTS
  butter, for greasing
  900g/2lb sweet potatoes
  115g/4oz/½ cup soft light
    brown sugar
  30ml/2 tbsp lemon juice
  45ml/3 tbsp butter
  4 strips smoked lean bacon, cut
    into matchsticks
  salt and ground black pepper
  1 flat leaf parsley sprig, to garnish

1 Preheat the oven to 190°C/375°F/
Gas 5 and lightly butter a shallow
ovenproof dish. Cut each unpeeled
sweet potato crosswise into three and
cook in boiling water, covered, for about
25 minutes until just tender.

2 Drain and leave to cool. When cool
enough to handle, peel and slice thickly.
Arrange in a single layer, overlapping
the slices, in the prepared dish.

3 Sprinkle over the sugar and lemon
juice and dot with butter.

4 Top with the bacon and season well.
Bake uncovered for 35–40 minutes,
basting once or twice.

5 The potatoes are ready once they are
tender, test them with a knife to make
sure. Remove from the oven once they
are cooked.

6 Preheat the grill to a high heat.
Sprinkle the potatoes with parsley. Place
the pan under the grill for 2–3 minutes
until the potatoes are browned and the
bacon is crispy. Serve hot.

SWEET POTATO FISH ROLLS

THE SWEETNESS OF THE POTATOES IS OFFSET PERFECTLY BY THE TARTNESS OF THE LEMON BUTTER SAUCE SERVED OVER THE FISH ROLLS.

SERVES FOUR

INGREDIENTS
   2 large sweet potatoes
   450g/1lb cod fillet
   300ml/½ pint/1¼ cups milk
   300ml/½ pint/1¼ cups water
   30ml/2 tbsp chopped parsley
   rind and juice of 1 lemon
   2 eggs, beaten
For the coating
   175g/6oz/3 cups fresh white
      breadcrumbs
   5ml/1 tsp Thai 7-spice seasoning
   vegetable oil, for frying
For the sauce
   50g/2oz/4 tbsp butter
   150ml/¼ pint/⅔ cup single cream
   15ml/1 tbsp chopped fresh dill
   lemon zest, to serve

1 Scrub the sweet potatoes and cook them in their skins in plenty of lightly salted boiling water for 45 minutes or until very tender. Drain and cool.

2 When the potatoes are cool, peel the skins and mash the flesh.

3 Place the cod fillet in a large frying pan and pour over the milk and water. Cover and poach for 10 minutes or until the fish starts to flake.

4 Drain and discard the milk, and then remove the skin and the bones from the fish.

5 Flake the fish into the potatoes in a large bowl, stir in the parsley, the rind and juice of ½ of the lemon and 1 egg. Chill for 30 minutes.

COOK'S TIP
Make sure the mixture is chilled thoroughly before you begin shaping and cooking. This helps to hold the ingredients together.

6 Divide and shape the mixture into 8 oval sausages. Dip each in egg. Mix the breadcrumbs with the seasoning. Roll the dipped fish rolls in the breadcrumbs.

7 Heat the oil and shallow fry in batches for about 7 minutes, carefully rolling the rolls to brown evenly. Remove from the pan and drain on kitchen paper. Keep hot.

8 To make the sauce, melt the butter in a small pan and add the remaining lemon juice and rind and allow the mixture to sizzle for a few seconds.

9 Remove from the heat and add the cream and dill. Whisk well to prevent the sauce from curdling and serve with the fish rolls.

SPICED SWEET POTATO TURNOVERS

*THE SUBTLE SWEETNESS OF THESE WONDERFUL PINK "POTATOES" MAKES A GREAT TURNOVER FILLING
WHEN FLAVOURED WITH A SELECTION OF LIGHT SPICES.*

SERVES FOUR

INGREDIENTS

For the filling

    1 sweet potato, about 225g/8oz
    30ml/2 tbsp vegetable oil
    2 shallots, finely chopped
    10ml/2 tsp coriander seeds, crushed
    5ml/1 tsp ground cumin
    5ml/1 tsp garam masala
    115g/4oz/1 cup frozen petit pois,
     thawed
    15ml/1 tbsp chopped fresh mint
    salt and ground black pepper
    mint sprigs, to garnish

For the pastry

    15ml/1 tbsp olive oil
    1 small egg
    150ml/¼ pint/⅔ cup natural yogurt
    115g/4oz/8 tbsp butter, melted
    275g/10oz/2½ cups plain flour
    1.5ml/¼ tsp bicarbonate of soda
    10ml/2 tsp paprika
    5ml/1 tsp salt
    beaten egg, to glaze

1 Cook the sweet potato in boiling salted water for 15–20 minutes, until tender. Drain well and leave to cool. When cool enough to handle, peel the potato and cut into 1cm/½in cubes.

2 Heat the oil in a frying pan, add the shallots and cook until softened. Add the sweet potato and fry until it browns at the edges. Add the spices and fry, stirring, for a few seconds. Remove the pan from the heat and add the peas, mint and seasoning to taste. Leave to cool.

3 Preheat the oven to 200°C/400°F/ Gas 6. Grease a baking sheet. To make the pastry, whisk together the oil and egg, stir in the yogurt, then add the melted butter. Sift the flour, bicarbonate of soda, paprika and salt into a bowl, then stir into the yogurt mixture to form a soft dough. Turn out the dough, and knead gently. Roll it out, then stamp it out into rounds.

4 Spoon about 10ml/2 tsp of the filling on to one side of each round, then fold over and seal the edges.

5 Re-roll the trimmings and stamp out more rounds until the filling is used up.

6 Arrange the turnovers on the prepared baking sheet and brush the tops with beaten egg. Bake in the oven for about 20 minutes until crisp and golden brown. Serve hot, garnished with mint sprigs.

ORANGE CANDIED SWEET POTATOES

A TRUE TASTE OF AMERICA, NO THANKSGIVING OR CHRISTMAS TABLE IS COMPLETE UNLESS SWEET POTATOES ARE ON THE MENU. SERVE WITH EXTRA ORANGE SEGMENTS TO MAKE IT REALLY SPECIAL.

SERVES EIGHT

INGREDIENTS

900g/2 lb sweet potatoes
250ml/8 fl oz/1 cup orange juice
50ml/2fl oz/¼ cup maple syrup
5ml/1 tsp freshly grated ginger
7.5ml/1½ tsp ground cinnamon
6.5ml/1¼ tsp ground cardamom
7.5ml/1½ tsp salt
ground black pepper
ground cinnamon, to garnish
orange segments, to serve

1 Preheat the oven to 180ºC/350ºF/Gas 4. Peel and dice the potatoes and then boil in water for 5 minutes.

2 Meanwhile, stir the remaining ingredients together. Spread out onto a non-stick shallow baking tin.

3 Drain the potatoes and scatter over the tray, cook for 1 hour, stirring the potatoes every 15 minutes until the potatoes are tender and they are well coated. Serve as a accompaniment to a main dish, with orange segments and ground cinnamon.

SWEET POTATO AND HONEY BREAD ROLLS

A SWEET ROLL THAT TASTES AS DELICIOUS SERVED WITH CONSERVES AS WITH A SAVOURY SOUP.

MAKES TWELVE

INGREDIENTS
  1 large sweet potato
  225g/8oz/2 cups strong white flour
  5ml/1 tsp easy-blend dried yeast
  pinch ground nutmeg
  pinch cumin seeds
  5ml/1 tsp runny honey
  200ml/7fl oz/scant 1 cup
    lukewarm milk
  oil, for greasing

1 Cook the potato in plenty of boiling water for 45 minutes or until very tender. Preheat the oven to 220°C/425°F/Gas 7.

2 Meanwhile, sift the flour into a large bowl, add the yeast, ground nutmeg and cumin seeds. Give the ingredients a good stir.

3 Mix the honey and milk together. Drain the potato and peel the skin. Mash the potato flesh and add to the flour mixture with the liquid.

4 Bring the mixture together and knead for 5 minutes on a floured surface. Place the dough in a bowl and cover with a damp cloth. Leave to rise for 30 minutes.

5 Turn the dough out and knock back to remove any air bubbles. Divide the dough into 12 pieces and shape each one into a round.

6 Place the rolls on a greased baking sheet. Cover with a damp cloth and leave to rise in a warm place for 30 minutes or until doubled in size.

7 Bake for 10 minutes. Remove from the oven and drizzle with more honey and cumin seeds before serving.

COOK'S TIP
This dough is quite sticky, so use plenty of flour on the surface when you are kneading and rolling it.

SWEET POTATO SCONES

THESE ARE SCONES WITH A DIFFERENCE. A SWEET POTATO GIVES THEM A PALE ORANGE COLOUR AND THEY ARE MELTINGLY SOFT IN THE CENTRE, JUST WAITING FOR A KNOB OF BUTTER.

2 In a separate bowl, mix the mashed sweet potatoes with the milk and melted butter or margarine. Beat well to blend.

3 Add the flour to the sweet potato mixture and stir to make a dough. Turn out on to a lightly floured surface and knead until soft and pliable.

MAKES ABOUT TWENTY-FOUR

INGREDIENTS
butter, for greasing
150g/5oz/1¼ cups plain flour
20ml/4 tsp baking powder
5ml/1 tsp salt
15g/½oz/1 tbsp soft light
  brown sugar
150g/5oz mashed sweet potatoes
150ml/¼ pint/⅔ cup milk
50g/2oz/4 tbsp butter or margarine,
  melted

1 Preheat the oven to 230°C/450°F/ Gas 8. Grease a baking sheet. Sift together the flour, baking powder and salt into a bowl. Mix in the sugar.

4 Roll or pat out the dough to a 1cm/½in thickness. Cut into rounds using a 4cm/1½in cutter.

5 Arrange the rounds on the baking sheet. Bake for about 15 minutes until risen and lightly golden. Serve warm.

SWEET POTATO MUFFINS WITH RAISINS

MUFFINS HAVE BEEN A PART OF THE AMERICAN BREAKFAST FOR MANY YEARS. THIS VARIETY MIXES THE GREAT COLOUR AND FLAVOUR OF SWEET POTATOES WITH THE MORE USUAL INGREDIENTS.

2 Meanwhile, preheat the oven to 220°C/425°F/Gas 7. Sift the flour and baking powder over the potatoes with a pinch of salt and beat in the egg.

3 Stir the butter and milk together and pour into the bowl. Add the raisins and sugar and mix the ingredients until everything has just come together.

MAKES TWELVE

INGREDIENTS
    1 large sweet potato
    350g/12oz/3 cups plain flour
    15ml/1 tbsp baking powder
    1 egg, beaten
    225g/8oz/1 cup butter, melted
    250ml/8fl oz/1 cup milk
    50g/2oz/scant ½ cup raisins
    50g/2oz/¼ cup caster sugar
    salt
    12 paper muffin cases
    icing sugar, for dusting

1 Cook the sweet potato in plenty of boiling water for 45 minutes or until very tender. Drain the potato and when cool enough to handle peel off the skin. Place in a large bowl and mash well.

4 Spoon the mixture into muffin cases set in a muffin tin.

5 Bake for 25 minutes until golden. Dust with icing sugar and serve warm.

INDEX

ACKNOWLEDGEMENTS

Of the many people and organisations
who have patiently answered questions
Alex Barker and the publishers would like
to thank the following:
Three Countries Potatoes, (David
Chappel of Newport, Norman Hosking of
Penzance, Morrice Innes of
Aberdeenshire and Andrew McQueen of
Shrewsbury) – especially for providing so
many potato samples for photography;
Alan Wilson (Agronomist and Potato
Specialist to Waitrose) and *The Story of
the Potato* by Alan Wilson published by
Alan Wilson; Alan Romans – and his
Guide to Seed Potato Varieties published
by the Henry Doubleday Research
Organisation, Ryton Organic Gardens,
Coventry CV8 3LG UK; David Turnbull
and Stuart Carnegie at the Scottish
Agricultural Science Agency; Nicola Bark
of Vegfed, Huddart Parker Building, Post
Office Square, PO Box 10232,
Wellington, New Zealand Tel 644472
3795 Fax 644471 2861
www.vegfed.co.nz; Lori Wing, The Potato
Association of America, University of
Maine, 5715 Coburn Hall, #6 Orono, ME
04469 5715; Kathleen Haynes
@asrr.arsusda.gov, Dr Alvin Reeves
REEVES@ MAINE.MAINE.EDU; Carl
Duivenvoorden, New Brunswick

Agriexport Inc., 850 Lincoln Rd PO Box
1101, Station "A", Fredericton, New
Brunswick, Canada E3B 5C2 Tel 506
453 2890 Fax 506 453 7170; Peter
Boswall, Prince Edward Island
Agriculture & Forestry, PO Box 1600,
Charlottetown, Prince Edward Island,
Canada CIA 7N3 Tel 902 368 5600 Fax
902 368 5729; An Bord Glas, 8–11
Lower Baggot Street, Dublin 2; Dr F Ezeta
and Christine Graves, The International
Potato Centre, Lima, Peru; The British
Potato Council, 4300 Nash Court, John
Smith Drive, Oxford Business Park,
South, Oxford OX4 2RT; Phil Harlock at
Covent Garden Supply Co., A24–29 New
Covent Garden Market, London SW8
5LR; Colin Randel, Mr Fothergill's Seeds,
Kentford, Newmarket, Suffolk CB8 7QB
Tel 01638 751 161 Fax 01638 751 624.
Not forgetting the many other companies,
farmers, producers and experts
worldwide who have helped answer my
numerous questions.

For potato samples for photography:
Glens of Antrim Potatoes, Red Bay,
Cushendall, Co Antrim, BT44 0SH;
ASDA; J Sainsbury plc; Waitrose
For the loan of photographic props:
David Mellor, 4 Sloane Square, London

SW1 Tel 020 7730 4259; Divertimenti,
139–141 Fulham Rd, London SW3 6SD
Mail Order 020 8246 4300; Elizabeth
David Cookshop, Covent Garden, London
WC2 Tel 020 7836 9167; Kenwood Ltd,
New Lane, Havant, Hampshire PO9 2NH
Tel 02392 476000; Magimix UK Ltd,
115A High Street, Godalming, Surrey
GU7 1AQ Tel 01483 427 411

For her styling, hand modelling and days
of researching – Stephanie England.

Useful reference publications:
*The Netherlands Catalogue of Potato
Varieties* 1997, published by NIVAA
The Potato Variety Handbook published
by NIAB (The National Institute of
Agricultural Botany) Huntingdon Rd,
Cambridge CB3 0LE UK
Potato Varieties in Canada 1997,
produced by the New Brunswick
Department of Agriculture, Canada
*Classification of Potato Varieties in the
Reference Collection at East Craigs,
Edinburgh*, by Douglas M Macdonald,
published by the Scottish Office
Agriculture and Fisheries Department
Atlantic Canada Potato Guide published
by authority of the Atlantic Provinces
Agriculture Services Co-ordinating

Committee, New Brunswich, Canada
*EC Common Catalogue Vol 40, (Plant
Varieties and Seeds Gazette)* from The
Stationery Office Ltd, 51 Nine Elms,
London SW8 4DR
*North American Potato Varieties
Handbooks* published by the Potato
Association of America

Picture Credits:
All pictures taken by Steve Moss
(potatoes and techniques), Sam Stowell
(recipes) and Walt Chrynwski (US
potatoes) except for the following: p. 6
(top and bottom, p. 7 (top), p. 8 E.T.
Archive; p. 7 (bottom) Illustrated London
News; p. 9 (bottom) The British Potato
Council; p. 10 (middle and bottom) The
International Potato Centre, Peru.

NOTES

NOTES

NOTES

NOTES